WENDY GIMBEL

Havana Dreams

Wendy Gimbel made many childhood visits to the
family of her paternal grandmother in pre-Castro
Cuba. She later went on to receive a Ph.D. in English
literature, and is the author of a scholarly book on
Edith Wharton. Her articles have appeared in *The
New York Times*, *Vogue*, *Mirabella*, *The Nation*, and
other publications. She has two grown sons and lives
with her husband in New York City.

Havana Dreams

WENDY GIMBEL

Havana Dreams

A Story of a Cuban Family

VINTAGE BOOKS

A Division of Random House, Inc.

New York

FIRST VINTAGE BOOKS EDITION, MAY 1999

The Library of Congress has cataloged the Knopf book as follows:

Gimbel, Wendy
Havana dreams: a story of cuba / Wendy Gimbel. —1st ed.
p.   cm.
ISBN 0-679-43053-9
I. Revuelta Clews, Natalia, 1925– .   2. Castro, Fidel, 1927–
—Relations with women.   3. Fernandez Revuelta, Alina, 1956– .
4. Cuba—History—1933–1959.   5. Cuba—History—1959–.
6.Mistresses—Cuba—Biography.
I.Title.
F1788.22.B47G56 1998
972.9106 4 092—dc21   98-14571
[B] CIP

Vintage ISBN: 0-679-75070-3

Author photograph © Marion Ettlinger

www.randomhouse.com/vintage

Printed in the United States of America
10 9 8 7 6 5 4 3 2 1

For my husband, Doug,
and my sons, David and Mark

Havana Dreams

The dream is a cocktail at Sloppy Joe's—
(Maybe—nobody knows.)

The dream is the road to Batabanó.
(But nobody knows if that is so.)

Perhaps the dream is only her face—
Perhaps it's a fan of silver lace—
Or maybe the dream's a Vedado rose—
(*Quién sabe?* Who really knows?)

—*Langston Hughes*

CONTENTS

Havana Dreams

PROLOGUE

PERHAPS the indifference in the face of the customs man when I announced the reason for my visit—a search for my grandmother's Cuba—should have warned me I might not find it. History, after all, had transformed her beloved country into a strange, unfamiliar place. But even if Cuba hadn't been different, the island to which she had taken me as a child had splintered, in my memory, into fragments of images: an aunt's white house, lustrous in the sunlight, a curved iron grille; fanlights, carmine and cobalt blue; a dense garden shaded with Indian laurel, a refuge where I felt loved, secure. But I, too, had changed and become someone else. The sun-drenched island my grandmother and I had known together was as irrecoverable to me as the Cuba of Spanish galleons, silver buckles, and golden doubloons.

My early Cuban adventure resulted from a very American childhood. My parents, who lived in New York City, had started out as the sort of couple that made people think of romantic comedies—an attractive Vassar graduate descended from New England Congregational ministers, and a handsome dreamer from Cuba—a man with pale-blue eyes, whose ancestors were careful merchants from Barcelona.

They fell in love with each other, or thought they had. More probably, my father was infatuated with my mother's good looks, her energy and brains. When he looked at her, he thought he saw America; my mother's romance was with Europe and the Caribbean, with noble causes, the Spanish Civil War, and the dream of a better world. Two years after they met, my parents married.

It must have seemed a glamorous marriage—the parties, the long evenings with writers and artists—Ernest Hemingway, Sherwood Anderson, the painter Rufino Tamayo—and the exiled leaders of the Spanish Republic. But my father, who had once found my mother charming, soon thought her brittle and superficial; meanwhile, she began to find him tedious, too serious. The marriage hurtled backwards to its predictable end.

I was not even a year old when my mother fell in love with another man, and my small, private universe fell apart. Although I was too young to remember the cold, black moment of abandonment, I was defined through that experience—one that would lend a particular emotional texture to my childhood.

As a little girl in the forties and fifties, I rarely saw either of my parents. My mother had left me behind—in New York City, where I was born—when she ended her marriage to my father. He had vanished as well—World War II had just ended—and had gone to Lisbon on a mission for the State Department. From Portugal, he sent me many dolls: folk dolls made of white yarn and dressed in bright-red aprons. They came in pairs like other people's parents. *¡Qué muñecas tan lindas!* everyone said. What perfectly beautiful dolls! *El debe quererte mucho.* He must love you very much.

My Cuban grandmother, a melancholy woman with a will of steel, determined to separate me forever from these two frivolous people who had grown tired of each other. Her judgment of my mother was particularly severe. What could be said of a woman so selfish that she could fall in love with another man, leave her husband, and abandon her daughter forever? As compensation, or, perhaps, restitution, for the painful exile into which she believed my mother had delivered me, my grandmother decided that for part of each year, we would leave New York and visit her family in Cuba. *¡Que niña más linda!* my Cuban aunts and cousins would chorus. What a beautiful child! *Sabes que la madre—una americana—la abandonó.* (Her mother, you know—an American woman—abandoned her.)

My mother's family—formal Bostonians who loved Emerson's essays and Sargent's paintings—sent me Christmas cards, scarves and gloves on birthdays, but I almost never saw them. I was often told that, when my mother had announced her future plans to Uncle Willie, the family patriarch, he had thundered: "How dare you do this to your daughter? Where is Wendy?" Willard Gardner Sperry, Dean of the Harvard Divinity School, Plummer Professor of Christian Morals, had no tolerance for a niece who had sacrificed her marriage and an infant child to follow the heady course of her passions.

Hadn't I, after all, been hijacked by my father's family? In Cuba, aunts and cousins chattered about me as they played mah-jongg. Their own lives were languid games played under the old, traditional rules. I must have been almost an adolescent when I first began to understand that, to my Cuban relatives, I was a wild card with a foreign design which had suddenly appeared in a familiar deck. From where they sat, it seemed impossible to play with such a card, but they were affectionate enough to try. *María Gloria tenía toda la razón en traerla a Cuba.* My grandmother—or so they believed—had every good reason to take me to Cuba.

. . .

IN THE middle of the nineteenth century, my grandmother's father, Don Jacinto Alsina, emigrated from Barcelona to Santiago, Cuba, where he managed to secure a comfortable fortune in sugar. Around 1880 he married María Josefa de la Presilla (Mamá Alsina, as everyone called her when she was elderly), the daughter of a prosperous sugar planter—a pampered, headstrong young woman who had first seen the light at Las Peladas, her grandfather's vast plantation outside the city of Santiago. At Las Peladas, the slaves cut the sugar cane, the women embroidered handkerchiefs, and the men occupied themselves with rum and cigars.

But in 1868, during the island's unsuccessful bid for independence from Spain (a relative of Mamá Alsina, Carlos Manuel de Céspedes, was the leader of the rebel movement), Cuban soldiers torched Las Peladas and burned the house to the ground. Mamá Alsina's father, uncompromising in his support of Spain, had become an emblem of the hated colonial establishment. As Las Peladas crumbled, Mamá Alsina was carried to safety astride a horse-drawn cannon. Even when I knew her, as a very old woman, she remembered the smoke and the terrible noise. I imagined how she must have looked as she fled the fire, a frightened child in a white dress, her own poignant battle costume.

After his marriage, Don Jacinto bought himself Central Sofía, a sugar refinery situated between the provincial towns of Manzanillo and Vega, in the province of Oriente: there, the New World odyssey of his family began. He prospered and bought several *fincas*, ranches, where he raised cattle and some of the cane that Sofía would grind each year. Even after the refinery had to be sold—my great-grandfather's sons, irresponsible gamblers, couldn't see it through the global sugar crisis of the thirties—the family's romance centered on Sofía.

Everyone remembered it not as land and property but as a capricious aunt who had loved and indulged them.

Born in Santiago, into a Spanish, colonial world, Don Jacinto's daughter, my grandmother, was a proper Victorian woman—someone who found comfort in conventional behavior, and strength in social rigidities. When she was a child and practiced the piano, the teacher had fastened an iron rod to her spine, to insure proper posture. Trained to honor her father, she did the same with her husband, becoming the devoted, uncomplaining wife of a difficult Spaniard whom she followed to Barcelona and, later, to New York City. But she lived, in her mind, in a romantic vision of Cuba, an Eden to which she returned each winter, more often than not with the granddaughter it had fallen to her to raise.

WHEN I first arrived in Cuba with my grandmother, much of the family's land was gone and with it the sense of adventure. The large, affectionate clan that embraced me were, for the most part, contented bourgeoisie in Santiago. The aunts doused themselves with Guerlain and worried about heart palpitations in the heat. The children chased each other in tiled patios filled with sunlight; we ate the sour-sweet fruit that hung from the mamoncillo branches. Sometimes I found a secret store of *dulce de leche,* a blancmange so sweet it made me shudder as I rolled it around my tongue. In the evenings, the little girls became marionettes in starched pastel dresses, paraded before a chorus of admiring adults.

María Elena. Por favor, siéntate bien. (Please, María Elena, sit still.) Each afternoon, my cousin María Elena sat at her mother's dressing table. I loved to watch her mother plaiting María Elena's thick black hair into long braids and fastening them with grosgrain ribbons. As soon as her mother was out of sight, María Elena loosened her hair, sending it tumbling across her face. But each morning, the ceremony began again, and I noticed that María Elena's mother seemed to love her as much as ever, no matter what she'd done to her braids.

When she went out for the evening, María Elena's mother would lean over to kiss us both, leaving her daughter's bedroom filled with the scent of her perfume. I remember closing my eyes, pretending that the perfume came from my own mother, not hers. That was sometimes. More often, I sold my absent mother down the river. I pretended that I was María Elena, and that her warm, scented, laughing mother belonged to me. When I think about that time, the pleasure comes from those moments of affection in what seemed to me then the most blessed of places.

WHEN I first returned to Havana as an adult, in 1991, I visited Tía Antonia's house. My great-aunt had died, but I thought her presence might be hovering over the orange trees or behind the bougainvillea in her beloved garden. Instead, as I looked through the iron gate, I could see in front of the massive wooden doors a pair of soldiers standing at attention, visiting military officers from Vietnam—a country Tía Antonia would have known as Indochina. The brilliant, radiant garden, now paved with cement, had been turned into a miniature parade ground where the soldiers saluted and marched.

The Vietnamese soldiers at Tía Antonia's house bivouacked in the ruins of the past, among shattered columns and broken furniture. The island that these soldiers harbored inside themselves had nothing to do with the Eden she had known. Everything seemed to have changed—everything but the green lizards that climbed on the walls of the ancient house. From the hills of the Sierra Maestra, Fidel had come thundering down, diverting the country from its predictable course, sending its people scattering in all directions.

Too often, families had fractured and ended up hurling insults at each other across the Florida straits. Both *los gusanos* (the "worms," as Castro called them, who had gone from the island) and *los comunistas* (those who remained behind) seemed to be nothing more than stubborn foot soldiers in clashing armies. Once again, as so long ago, I was a visitor, an outsider. But now Fidel Castro hovered over the grave of the world I had known with my grandmother.

Every story had at its center a single political event: the success of one man and his revolution. As in so many other unfortunate countries, history had had a dramatic and severe effect on ordinary life. Every family in Cuba had suffered in the revolution: emotional structures crumbled; friends and relatives were driven into exile. No one on the island was able to swerve far enough to avoid a collision with Fidel Castro. It was nostalgia, then, and the sense of emptiness that came to me as I observed this now battered island, that compelled me to find a way to understand it.

Some people look at architecture—cathedrals with vaulted ceilings, thatched cottages on a country lane—and emerge with a sense of place. Others chase butterflies, paint wildflowers, or observe flora in the rain forest to form an impression of their environment. (I am married to a lawyer who arrives in another country, locates the nearest courthouse, and eagerly awaits a trial he can watch from the visitors' gallery.) But family remains the lens through which I look at the world. When I want to read a culture, I listen to stories about families, sensing in their contours the substance of larger mysteries.

While in Havana, I was introduced to a Cuban family— three generations of women (four, counting the youngest in the line, a girl of fifteen when I met her). Descendants of settlers from Spain and England, these were women whose lives had spanned the twentieth century on the island. Through their intertwining narratives, it occurred to me that I might construct a telling story of Cuba.

My own family had packed up the paintings, buried the silver, and fled the island immediately after the revolution, delivering themselves into the history of other countries. But Natalia Revuelta and her mother, daughter, and granddaughter had so far remained in place, withstanding all the economic turmoil and the political convulsions that had made the island tremble for the last hundred years. One generation followed another, each imprinted with a part of the island's poignant tale. And this particular family, more literally than most, had reflected Fidel Castro's seduction of Cuba.

Naty Revuelta's mother, Doña Natica, who was over ninety when I first met her, was born into a Cuba that had recently belonged to Spain. Naty herself, born in 1925, was educated in Washington, D.C., and Philadelphia. She started out as a socialite during the Batista era, married a prominent cardiologist, and became intoxicated with the romance of Fidel Castro and his revolution. Soon after Fidel's victory, Naty's husband and elder daughter, Nina, followed thousands of disillusioned Cubans into exile. Naty remained in Havana with her second child, Alina Fernández Revuelta, who was born in 1956. Alina seemed to me to mirror the disillusionment of the country as its Communist infrastructure unraveled. Her young daughter, Mumín (pronounced Moo-MEEN), a dancer, embodied the promise of the future as the island approached the millennium.

The first time I saw Naty, Doña Natica, and Alina together, it was late in the evening. Outside the large gray house, the insistent chant of cicadas blended with the smell of jasmine. Inside a lightless room, the black-and-white television framed the image of Fidel—a man whose voice thrusted energy into the walls. Present as he was, in a contained electronic quadrangle, Fidel reminded me of the absent father in a daguerreotype: the mother, surrounded by her children in their Sunday best, poses with a photograph of her husband. His presence in the portrait confirms his position as the source of well-being in the family.

But here, something was strange. This particular group—three women and a bearded dictator in a rectangular box—suggested not closeness but dissociation and estrangement. Fidel Castro, now a tremoring, aging patriarch, might have been the respected head of such a family. But there was no connection between this man and the women in the room. The elderly Doña Natica closed her eyes and ignored the television set. She seemed not to hear Fidel as he railed against the United States. Alina turned her back to the reflected image. Only Naty stared intently at the screen, although her dream, too, had begun to fade, and the remembered past must have filled her soul with flint.

CHAPTER I

Havana,
Before and After

ON THE morning of July 10, 1555—as the sun rose over the entrance to a narrow harbor—the honorable Juan de Lobera, mayor of Havana, was a very worried man. The French corsair Jacques de Sores had landed on the island of Cuba, just outside de Lobera's small settlement. With his band of marauders, de Sores approached the village on foot. (Chroniclers claim that they violated some poor, frightened priests they'd met along the way, and then rode them around as though they were horses.) In no time at all—it took just thirty minutes, according to historians—the governor fled the island and the pirates took the town.

Jacques de Sores, an ambitious buccaneer not easily satisfied, craved the precious cargo rescued from the wrecks of Spanish galleons that had sunk in the fierce hurricanes off the island's coast. A cunning pirate, he had no doubt that he would find the riches stored in the Castillo Real de la Fuerza, a bleak fortress overlooking the harbor.

For de Sores, storming the vulnerable castle proved no problem, but absconding with the treasure turned out to be more difficult than he might have dreamed. Arrogant, confident of his strength, the pirate had considered the favorable odds, but he had not counted on the single-minded tenacity of Mayor Juan de Lobera. With a few frightened settlers, the stubborn Spaniard had barricaded himself inside the castle, and there he remained, refusing to surrender.

Furious at his stubborn, intractable foe, an exhausted de Sores had no recourse but to sack the town of Havana and burn it to the ground. One can only imagine, after all that trouble, how frustrating it must have been for the pirate to discover, when he entered La Fuerza, that it contained no treasure at all. Juan de Lobera had resisted, it seems, not because he was guarding a treasure, but because it was his destiny

Returning to Havana in the early 1990s, I thought the city might be replicating this strange, isolated moment in its history. Fidel Castro, holding out against all odds, was standing fast in his citadel; the Cuban people, caught inside his fortress, had no choice but to go along with him and wait for the future to reveal itself. What was certain was that there was treasure—and it wasn't hard to rescue. Havana's wealth was in the narratives, the individual stories woven through its four-hundred-year history. I couldn't have known then what would happen when I opened the treasure chest, held a single story up to the light.

WHEN Christopher Columbus sailed from Spain in 1492, he believed that the currents would take him as far as the court of the Mongol emperors. It never occurred to him that a huge continent stood in his path. The world was larger than the Italian mariner had thought, and instead of the fabled land of precious stones, of lustrous pearls and fragrant spices, he found himself in the Bahamas. It was there that he first heard of a treasure island, one he thought Marco Polo might have visited.

In the belief that he could reach this marvelous Eden, Columbus sailed south, and then west, until he finally landed in Cuba.

For the exuberant explorer, his head swirling with dreams of riches, of Marco Polo's treasure island or the fabulous empire of Cathay, it was difficult to find himself on an island of tobacco-smoking Taino living in miserable thatched huts. In fact, Columbus insisted that his men sign an oath—on pain of having their tongues excised—swearing that Cuba was not an island but part of the mainland of China. It took him a while to settle into the position of a clever merchant intent upon exploiting his commercial position: "Where there is such marvelous scenery," he wrote in a letter to his patrons, Ferdinand and Isabella of Spain, "there must be much from which profit can be made."

Other Spaniards intent on profit soon followed. The brutal conquistador Diego Velázquez mined the island for gold, massacred the Indians, and fed himself on parrots. Hernando de Soto—a man who had climbed mountains in Peru, crossed faltering bridges that stretched across gigantic chasms, and stormed the Inca warriors in the square of Caxamarca—came to the island on another search for the elusive "El Dorado." But in Cuba there was very little of the precious metal; most of it was in the minds of the ruthless explorers.

Sebastián de Ocampo, an ordinary soldier with a practical nature, determined that Cuba could be valuable to Spain, even if nothing the conquistadors touched turned to gold. At the beginning of the sixteenth century, he founded Puerto Carenas—a sheltered natural-harbor town on the western side of the island, where the huge, cumbersome vessels sailing between Spain and the New World could be serviced and secured. In 1519, Puerto Carenas became San Cristóbal de La Habana, absorbing the name and population of the original Havana—

an unsuccessful settlement sixty miles farther along the coast. In 1624, the Spanish crown decreed the second Havana to be La Llave del Nuevo Mundo (The Key to the New World).

MORE than a hundred years before the Dutch founded New Amsterdam, Havana was thriving, hosting more than her fair share of dreamers, schemers, and reprobates. Like a palimpsest, this ancient city bears the traces of its earlier, imperfectly erased tales. Weaving together these narratives of greed and ambition, Havana's master tale reveals itself: *Treasure Island*, perhaps, crossed with *The Tempest*.

The tales of treasure hunters give Cuba's history an undulating, wavelike pattern. In all of these stories, Havana stands like a beacon at the edge of the sea, luring adventurers to her shores with the promise of fabulous riches: Spanish conquistadors, French buccaneers, the English Admiralty, American industrialists, and Mafia gangsters. The characters change, the costumes are different—say, the British in scarlet coats, the Las Vegas mobsters sporting pointed shoes and diamond rings—but the narrative remains the same. In Havana, everything that glitters turns to gold.

In the sixteenth century—and for more than a hundred years after that—Havana defended the very entrance to the Caribbean. The historian Antonio Benítez-Rojo, author of *The Repeating Island*, points out that without this "Caribbean machine"—the elaborate system of fleets, garrisons, and ports—the Spanish would have been in the absurd position of the gambler who hits the jackpot but has no hat in which to catch his winnings.

Pirates sailed for Havana because it was the gathering place for the Spanish treasure fleets—the regal, three-masted galleons which caught the tradewinds out of Seville, headed for the Spanish Main, collected the wealth of the Americas, and returned home across the Atlantic. Each year, carried by the great Atlantic currents, these huge "floating cities" sailed back and forth between Seville and the New World, breaking the journey in Havana.

Some of the galleons went to Veracruz and returned to Havana laden with Mexican gold and silver. Others went by way of the northern coasts of Panama, Colombia, and Venezuela. They carried mined gold and silver from Colombia and Peru, bales of cochineal, casks of indigo, chalices encrusted with emeralds and pearls. In Havana Harbor, the pirate-fearing galleons waited for each other—often there were more than a hundred ships in a *flota*—and, in an impressive convoy, caught the westerlies and sailed for Spain.

This storehouse for the fabled treasures of the Indies must have been a thrilling place for Jacques de Sores or any other self-respecting pirate. Imagine the bloodthirsty, arrogant buccaneers, their bravado as they prowled the seas outside the harbor ready to pounce: the Chevalier de Gramont, a Frenchman, feared by the Spanish for his cruelty to prisoners; England's Sir Francis Drake, who threatened to burn Havana to the ground but changed his mind and sailed, instead, for Roanoke, Virginia; Edward Teach, known as Blackbeard, who tied ribbons into his beard and wore lighted tapers protruding from under his hat.

On the high seas, the admiral of the treasure fleet gave formal banquets to which he invited guests from the other ships. While they dined on sweetmeats, everyone watched the more congenial passengers, including a rambunctious friar or two, performing the popular "cloak-and-dagger" comedies. Not that these festive events were without reminders that galleons were not palaces and that the Atlantic Ocean was not the Court of Madrid. Rats as large as rabbits often ate the biscuits and killed the parrots or the chickens long before the crew could hurl the birds from cages into cooking pots.

How amazing to have seen the majestic square-rigged galleons, with their enormous masts and topsails, appearing over the horizon! The people of Havana danced in the streets as though they were celebrating Carnival. The Spanish stocked the town with rare delicacies and imprinted the residents with sophisticated European manners and culture. From Spain to the New World they brought casks of wine, almonds, honey, and pimentos; bolts of velvet cloth, dancing monkeys, and the plays of Lope de Vega.

AFTER the Spanish explorers and the French pirates came the English sailors. In the seventeenth and eighteenth centuries, as Spain's power waned, Havana had every reason to fear a full-scale invasion by this next wave of adventurers. "When the greed of acquisition of territory is once roused in a nation," a contemporary historian has remarked, "it is difficult to appease it."

Though England's mercantile intent was to take any or all of the Spanish colonies, it was the great fortress cities of the Caribbean that had attracted her strategic gaze. Havana, a walled city with an impressive circle of forts, had become the greatest stronghold in the Americas. It would be the key to the New World for Great Britain as it had been for Spain.

In 1762, in a successful siege that lasted eleven months, the British took Havana. The Duke of Cumberland assured Lord Albemarle, the leader of the expedition, that everyone in England wished him to emerge from the action as rich as Croesus. "Health and owned merit are sufficient ingredients for happiness," asserted the practical Duke; "so much the better if you add wealth to it."

As always, Havana was more than accommodating to this intrusion of fortune hunters. Commodore Keppel, Albemarle's younger brother, demonstrated an enthusiasm for riches which was familiar even if his British mannerisms were not: "The Admiral has given us leave to take yonder town, with all the treasure in it; so we have nothing to do now, but make our fortune as fast as we can, for the place can never hold out against us. We shall all be as rich as Jews. The place is paved with gold."

Having more elaborate commercial fantasies than Jacques de Sores, the British weren't satisfied with the usual spoils of victory. Instead of succumbing to nostalgia for the gold and silver bursting from the holds of Spanish galleons, they set out to make their fortunes in the slave trade. Importing thousands of slaves from Dahomey, Lagos, and the Gold Coast, the British delivered a human cargo whose suffering created undreamed-of wealth. In the agony of this forced labor, the island began its transformation into a vast sugar plantation.

Historian Hugh Thomas, in *Cuba: The Pursuit of Freedom*, calls attention to William Cowper's "Pity for Poor Africans," the fashionable couplets in which an eighteenth-century Englishman justified his position on the slave trade:

> *I own I am shocked at the purchase of slaves*
> *And fear those who buy them and sell them are knaves;*
> *What I hear of their hardships, their tortures and groans,*
> *Is almost enough to draw pity from stones.*
> *I pity them greatly but I must be mum,*
> *For how could we do without sugar and rum.*

In 1763, signing the Peace of Paris, which ended the Seven Years' War between Spain, France, and England, the Spanish gave Florida to the British in exchange for Havana. At the time, most people thought that Spain's Charles III had gotten the better end of the real-estate deal.

THERE had been a sea change. Once a society of modest ranchers, artisans, and bureaucrats, Cuba had become a sugar-rich plantation society. Before the British siege of Havana, the island had been allowed to trade only with Spain; her surrender to the British had brought her her first experience with unhindered capitalism. Given the enormous number of slaves that Britain made available—and with greater markets—sugar production rose until, as historians point out, Cuba had become the most prosperous sugar colony in the world.

Throughout much of the nineteenth century, the *criollos*—the land-holding descendants of Spaniards who had come to the island during the preceding two hundred years—made great fortunes in sugar and emerged as an authentic island oligarchy. The social and political prominence of the *criollos* would outlive their future economic defeat at the hands of the Americans and the *recién llegados* (the recently arrived Spanish immigrants who succeeded them and became the early-twentieth-century nouveaux riches).

Antagonistic to the *peninsulares* (the native Spaniards), resistant to foreign designs on the island, the *criollos* were the earliest Cubans to harbor nationalist sentiments. Consider the history of *las damas de la Habana*—the *criollo* ladies who sold their precious gems to finance George Washington's victory over the despised English at the Battle of Yorktown. (These patriotic feelings against foreign domination hibernated during the time of the early Cuban republic but would awaken in the 1950s, when Fidel Castro decided to overthrow the American-backed government of General Batista.)

IT WAS the *criollos* who gave Havana a distinctive, sophisticated style. During the sugar harvest, they might visit their
plantations. But most of the time, they made their homes
within the walled town whose government and culture they
dominated. You can feel their presence in the gracious central
plazas, the fanciful *palacios, iglesias,* and *conventos.* Carved into
the entrances of their houses are their coats of arms—Pedroso,
Montalvo, O'Reilly, Beltrán de Santa Cruz y Aranda, Calvo de
la Puerta. . . . With their wealth, the *criollos* built magnificent
structures for themselves: palaces with immense grilled windows, stained-glass fanlights (*mediopuntos*), Andalusian tiles,
staircases of Italian marble, and patios ringed with frangipani
and ginger lily.

To amuse themselves, they gave formal balls, *bailes de eti-
queta,* danced the *contradanza habanera,* attended *conciertos* and
zarzuelas. At the end of the afternoon, they promenaded along
the tree-lined Paseo de Tacón. In the evening, they attended
the opera and the theatre (the Teatro de Tacón imported artists
from abroad), and yielded to the temptations of the gambling
casinos. In Havana, wrote a nineteenth-century traveler, "the
man of cultivated tastes" may revel in "a paradise of delights."

SLAVERY ended. With the sugar crisis of the 1880s, which
brought a plunge in the world market price of sugar, the debt-
ridden *criollos* found themselves on the edge of ruin. Vast
amounts of capital were needed to transform the slave-based
sugar business into a modern industry which relied on machines
to run the mills. It would come from the imperial Americans
with their fistfuls of cash—the last of the adventurers before
the coming of Fidel Castro.

Throughout the early decades of the twentieth century, the Americans not only bought and managed sugar plantations (including those in financial trouble, on which American banks were foreclosing), they also became the major market for Cuban sugar and the ultimate supplier of equipment for most of the plantations and mills, including the railroads that linked the plantations to the mills and the mills to the ports.

Listen, for example, to a story that's a paradigm—the tale of Central Soledad, a sugar plantation outside of Havana. In the beginning of the nineteenth century, Juan Sarriá, a Spaniard, had bought Soledad, an enormous tract of fertile land where hundreds of slaves planted and harvested the sugar cane. A savage, brutal ruler, Sarriá thought nothing of murdering his workers and flinging their bodies from the balconies of his hacienda. Domingo, his gentle son, renounced the rustic world of his father's plantations and graced the most decadent salons in Madrid. Juan's grandson, the dynasty's third generation, returned to Cuba to manage the Sarriá estates, but he was more accustomed to palaces than to the rough countryside. His thoroughbreds are said to have cantered on silver horseshoes. In the countryside, it was widely believed that Sarriá was a visiting prince.

A Bostonian whose father had sent him to Cuba on business, Edwin Atkins, came upon Soledad during the sugar crisis, when the Sarriás, like most planters, needed an infusion of capital. Before abolition, the slave traders had supplied all the cash; now the money for machinery to replace forced human labor would come from Americans, eager to invest in return for the deeds to valuable land.

"I can remember," wrote Atkins in a memoir, "when I first visited Soledad with José María Sarriá [Juan's grandson], I reined up my horse as we reached the top of the ridge that overlooks the *batey* and expressed admiration at the beautiful view of valley and mountain. 'It is yours,' said José María in the usual

Spanish formula. And I felt pretty sure it was, for I believed then that we should have to take possession to protect ourselves." As Atkins foreclosed on the Sarriás' mortgages, the torch was passing to a generation of Americans who believed in their own manifest destiny.

Edwin Atkins and his wife, Kathryn, were greeted at Soledad almost as divine rulers. He wrote: "We, the owners, sat upon a kind of throne constructed by the negroes and surrounded with the Spanish flag and coat-of-arms. . . . As the procession filed in front of us, many of the older African negroes would kneel and kiss our hands and feet, asking our blessing. . . ." In a few years, Edwin Atkins would transform the feudal Soledad into one of the largest modern sugar plantations in the world—twelve thousand acres, twenty-three miles of private railway, five thousand acres of cane.

I I

TO MEET the beautiful Naty Revuelta was to encounter a Cuban heroine in a state of siege. But I didn't know that yet. We met through a friend, an American woman, who knew I was interested in writing about the bourgeoisie who had remained in Havana. "Naty," she assured me, "knows everyone."

We had coffee at El Patio, a restaurant in Old Havana, once the palace of the Marqués de Aguas Claras. I couldn't have imagined Naty's enthusiasm, couldn't believe how generous she was with her time. I can still see her sitting opposite me, offering names and addresses, checking them against the penciled listings in a small, faded green alligator diary. "Wouldn't the CIA love to get their hands on this notebook," she had said, laughing.

The "everyone" Naty knew, it turned out, went beyond the bourgeoisie. In her youth, she had become enamored of the new Cuba. But unlike most people, she wasn't content to sit on the sidelines, to watch while events unfolded along the parade route. She already had the idea that she could break the rules with impunity—and she wanted to be a player.

Naty's beauty had always provided her with both entrée and absolution. Attracted with an almost magnetic pull to the edge of adventure, and operating within the mode she knew, she formed an intimate alliance with a bold young radical. Sitting in El Patio that afternoon, over many cups of Cuban coffee, Naty Revuelta told me about her romance with Fidel Castro.

After that, I went to her house. Overwhelmed by Naty, I was also intrigued by Doña Natica, Alina, and Mumín. It didn't take long for me to propose to Naty that I write about the Cuban generations of her family. White, middle-class, with forebears from Spain and England, they had arrived long before the revolution but after the age of the *criollos*. Thinking back to the beginnings of this undertaking, remembering my excitement about finding a story and the family's professed delight in being written about, I am surprised at the degree of our communal innocence. But it was true, at least when we started.

From the beginning, we got along well. Carefully guiding me through the streets, lamenting the vanished splendor, Naty seemed to have the same reactions I had to the humbled, crumbling city. Perhaps it wasn't so strange. We were talking about general things. Havana presented to everyone such a sustained image of resigned desperation—a place where everyone seemed to be waiting, but for what no one seemed to know. Juan de Lobera, Jacques de Sores, Fulgencio Batista, and Fidel Castro, locked in their own narratives, had played their historical roles. But what about ordinary Cubans caught inside the fortress, their destinies tied to those arrogant, narcissistic leaders?

Walking with Naty along the Paseo del Prado, where prerevolutionary *habaneros* once promenaded in the late afternoon, I found the silence troubling. It seemed louder than the remembered shouts of children playing, of vendors selling sweet oranges and *helado de ʒapote,* a sugary ice cream, of festive crowds filing into the Centro Gallego and the Teatro Nacional. The rustle of women's fans, I remember that, too—the rhythm set with the flick of a wrist holding the delicate *abanico.*

Along the streets that crisscross the city, people moved along on Chinese bicycles, in Russian Ladas, in pre-Castro Oldsmobiles and Pontiacs, in pastel Cadillacs with monster fins. Others, wearing stiletto heels or plastic sandals and holding empty shopping bags, waited hours for crowded buses that never came. Clutching their ration books, women waited in front of the government store for a few ounces of coffee, some rice and beans, a piece of fish.

Prowling dogs wandered through the streets, abandoned by their hungry owners. (The Cubans are not like the British; they can live without their dogs.) A friend of Naty's told me in confidence that a man was arrested for eating a neighbor's cat. Things got worse. The owner of the cat gave the thief the evil eye, causing him to have seizures and convulsions. When a man I met went to a dental clinic, the drills were broken and, of course, there was no anesthesia. Naty was waiting to have a doctor examine a tumor in her neck, but her turn hadn't come around. A woman whose hernia operation was not urgent was told to have the surgery while there was still thread to stitch her wound.

At the Hotel Riviera, where I stayed on one of my visits,

when you held the telephone receiver in your hand, you heard the strains of "Silent Night" instead of a dial tone. Sitting on a chair in front of the Hotel de Ambos Mundos, where Ernest Hemingway once lived, an old man in worn-out shoes looked through a tattered guide to Bulgaria. A graffiti artist crossed out the "o" from a poster and replaced it with "es." The sign that in Spanish had read "socialism or death" now read "socialism is death." But there is no deliverance.

"What is your fancy?" asked an American guidebook published more than fifty years earlier, in 1941. "Havana is like a woman in love. Eager to give pleasure, she will be anything you want her to be—exciting or peaceful, gay or quiet, brilliant or tranquil." "This isn't the real Havana," Naty reminds me. "You'll have to come back when all this is over."

Refracted through that wide lens, Havana, at the beginning of the nineties, seemed drab, and intolerable. Was the tale of this city a cautionary tale about power or a fable of resilience? How, in this poor, enervated place, did people manage to live? If I changed the lens, focusing more closely on particular individuals, it became clear that, to live in Havana, everyone had invented a strategy for survival. Those who hadn't budged from their homes had fled in their minds instead, and inhabited a more seductive, fantastical Havana.

ONE CUBAN friend of Naty's—an architect in love with each bend and curve of the city—inhabited a splendid, miniature Havana. When we visited him in his studio, he unveiled an intricate plaster model of the city—an ideal construction of perfect structures housed in an air-conditioned room, a Havana as immune to time as a marble statue in a mausoleum. The city in which he walked, the scale model through which he wandered with his wooden pointer, existed entirely out of the historical present.

At the point where his imagination intersected with the tiny buildings, the architect founded his glimmering city, or, rather, restored Havana to its romantic splendor: its stone houses built around patios filled with hibiscus, lemon, and pomegranate trees, its red-tiled roofs which reminded him of Cádiz, its ornate palaces with their arched *portales* and massive, intricately carved wooden doors.

Another of Naty's friends told me that he once watched a fisherman—a man intent on sailing to freedom across the Straits of Florida—as he constructed a boat that was nothing more than a floating oxcart. He made a bow of steel sheets from old washtubs and nailed them to a wooden frame; there was no stern, but there were two sails made of bedsheets. His passengers were to stand inside the boat, for the entire sail across the straits, as though they were sailors at attention, and forever under review. But the fisherman didn't see it as a madman's scheme. He used asphalt—there was no paint available—to paint "El Galeón" on the side of the raft, and then he sailed for the Florida Keys.

In the most ancient part of Havana, on the Calle Amargura (Bitterness Street), Raúl Macheco, a tall, slender black man just over fifty, celebrated his mass in a small room filled with yellow gladiolas. Statues of Santa Bárbara and the Virgen del Cobre hovered over the assembled followers. An *espiritista*—a medium who entered into a trance and became possessed with the spirit of the dead—he attracted attention with his fierce, manic energies. He arranged everyone in a circle, sprinkled them with sweet cologne, looked into a water glass as though it were a crystal ball, and called upon the dead "spirit" guardians to enter him.

Raúl Macheco's Yoruba ancestors, whom slave traders

brought in bondage to the island, had folded their sacred gods, the *orisha*, beneath the white man's Catholic saints, and released them again into the world as sacred energies. Macheco assigned salvation to the *babalaos* (high priests) and *santeros* (priests) while he called upon the dead to protect those stranded in Fidel's wasteland.

A man who needed to ransom himself from depression learned that his *muerto* (protective spirit) had predicted that he would come into a great fortune. A woman suffering from cancer heard that, if she made the sign of the cross while carrying a lighted candle, she would be cured: "You must not fear the dark, for the dark is the womb from which all life springs; neither must you fear the Night, for the Night is your friend, the bringer of rest," said the old *babalao:* "Learn to walk with the Night and she will be a good companion."

When Raúl offered his predictions, Naty bridled. "That's not for me," she said, recovering herself as we were leaving. I didn't give the incident a thought until much later, but then I found it in character. Naty hated situations in which she was at the mercy of someone else's narrative. "No," I would tell her more than once. "You can't read a draft of my book and make changes." "But," she would assure me, "I just want to make sure it's right."

It was a matter of temperament. On unfamiliar ground, without control, Naty became uneasy, tense and self-protective. At her daughter's suggestion, she had brought me to Macheco's *misa*, but she didn't want to participate or be observed by anyone. We both shared a fear of being thought vulnerable—indeed, ridiculous.

Some people were more comfortable with change. Natalia Bolívar Arostegui, a heavy-bosomed, energetic descendant of the *criollo* aristocracy, regarded Raúl as the closest of her friends. She wouldn't think of making a significant decision without consulting him. An anthropologist who writes and lectures on *santería* all over the world, Natalia has survived like some primordial amoeba, ingesting all the changes on the island.

Educated at the fashionable Convent of the Sacred Heart in Havana, and New York's Art Students League, this daughter of the oligarchy had turned from her debutante past and become a member of the student revolutionary movement at the University of Havana. Tortured by General Batista, disillusioned by Fidel, disgusted with the betrayal of the revolution, Natalia was still a vibrant part of her country's present.

The Arosteguis were a distinguished clan. (Because of their services to the Spanish crown, they had the special privilege of being allowed to ride horseback into the Cathedral of Havana.) At the end of the eighteenth century, Louis-Philippe, Duke of Orléans, fleeing the French Revolution, came to Cuba, where Martín Arostegui entertained him and lent him a great deal of money. When Louis-Philippe ascended the throne of France and tried to repay the debt, the gallant Arostegui replied that he had lent money to an exiled duke but not to the King of France. In gratitude, the monarch sent his Cuban friend a miniature painted by Jacques-Louis David, a likeness of the King's own beloved mother.

Nena Arostegui, Natalia's mother, thought nothing of calling the police when *un negro* sauntered along the streets in front of her house in the residential section of Miramar after dark. In the same house, which Natalia inherited—there are ten barking dogs living on the roof and several ex-husbands in the front parlor—she rules with the presence of an absolute monarch. *"Me quedo en Cuba por que pertenezco aquí. Pase lo que pase, es mi patria."* "I stay in Cuba because I belong here. Whatever happens, it's my homeland."

. . .

ACCORDING to Guillermo Jiménez, an amateur historian who fought with Fidel during the revolution, Natalia remained just because she *is* an old-fashioned aristocrat. A small, pale man with trembling hands, Guillermo had retreated into history in order to make sense of things. "If the wealthy, educated Cubans had remained in place," he says, "if they hadn't put on their jewelry and run to the United States for cover, the country could have gotten rid of Fidel Castro a long time ago." Decadent, self-indulgent, these Cubans were a far cry from the *criollos* of the last century, who had a sense of responsibility to the country, above all to its institutions, and would never have gone away. "Write down what I say for your book," he said. "It doesn't matter if everyone disagrees with me." *"Yo tengo que ser auténtico."* ("I have to be authentic.")

We got out of Naty's car in front of the decaying white house where the Suárez sisters, Elvira and Lilia, have sat out the revolution. How relieved she must have been that their world was so familiar. With some excitement in her voice, Naty said: "My father wanted to marry Elvira, so she's almost my mother." "These Suárez women," Naty said proudly, "wouldn't know what to make of *santería*. Don't mention Guillermo's attitude towards their friends who fled the country right after the fall of Batista."

Protective of these affectionate dowagers, Naty seemed at her best. For these aristocratic old ladies, immured among their remaining possessions, survival was in pretending that their prerevolutionary Cuba would come back. Since they never stepped out of their house, it was sometimes possible for the sisters to imagine that now was then. Soon they would be shopping at the French salon at El Encanto, packing their Vuitton trunks for their trips to Paris, attending the New Year's Eve party at the Vedado Tennis Club, or the Christmas tea dance at the Havana Yacht Club.

During their afternoon canasta games at the Yacht Club, the two sisters had traded anecdotes about *mulatos* who tried to pretend they were white. General Batista's suspicious racial bloodlines had earned him a blackball from the club's admissions committee, even though its action meant courting the anger of the vengeful chief of state. (The not-so-snobbish Havana Biltmore admitted the general and enjoyed the valuable real estate he gave to the members in gratitude.)

Elvira, who wore moth-eaten mauve silk, had the face of an elderly child—a pleasant girl astonished to find herself grown wrinkled and old. The afternoon canasta games to which she devoted herself began long before General Batista's coup d'état. Throughout the regime of Fidel Castro, her rhythm had remained the same: shuffle, deal, and discard. But with everyone leaving, it had become harder to find partners. Sometimes now, absent friends joined her in hands of imaginary canasta.

Lilia, perhaps the more reflective of the two relics, spent most of her afternoons with a magnifying glass, examining photographs of the family's lost *finca*—the ranch where she and her husband had ridden their thoroughbred horses. The gardens had been famous, but the Communists trampled on the orchids, killing the delicate plants. Could she find a photograph of the lovely crystal chandeliers, the most celebrated in Cuba? Or of those polished wooden floors from Barcelona, on which dancers whirled on balmy winter evenings?

Both sisters fretted about their possessions. When the revolution came, friends who were in the diplomatic service agreed to take the sisters' paintings out of the country. These ambassadors were never heard from again. In an effort to protect the valuables still in the house, Lilia had glued her Dresden figurines to the round tables in the entrance hall. She turned the tables upside down to demonstrate her cleverness. It looked, for all the world, as though the porcelain shepherds were dancing on their heads.

The decorative plates that hung on the wood-paneled walls of the dining room bore the coats of arms of *criollo* families. The Suárez family were proud of their descent from the Marqués de la Campiña, who came to Cuba with Christopher Columbus.

Lilia said: "My mother knew all about the noble families of Cuba. She knew which crest belonged to which family: the Montalvos, the Penalvers, the Pedrosos and Herreras. . . . There were so many, and she knew them all. We lost the piece of paper on which she'd written down the history of each title."

Elvira continued: "Some of our friends fled with nothing. They were leaving with one hand covering them in front and the other in back. But we couldn't imagine ourselves going to another country. Who would we have become without position, or without our possessions? We chose to believe, instead, that this would be over very soon." And now: *"Nos pasamos la vida viendo pasar el tiempo."* ("We spend our lives just watching time pass.")

For these two women, Fidel Castro's stranglehold on the island—a place from which he should have been banished decades ago—had no reasonable explanation. But nothing could be done about it. Finally, it came down to a matter of social position: "Fidel Castro's treatment of Naty Revuelta was terrible. It's because she lived in our world, one that wouldn't have accepted him." Lilia lowered her voice. *"Pero no pudo acabar con ella."* ("But he wasn't able to defeat her.")

CHAPTER 2

At Home with Naty Revuelta

Isle of Pines
November 7, 1953

Mrs. Natty [sic] Revuelta
Havana

Dear Natty,

A fond hello from my prison cell. Although it's been a while since I've heard from you, I remember you and love you very much. I keep and will always keep the affectionate letter which you sent to my mother. If you have suffered because of me, consider that, with pleasure, I would give my life for your honor and well-being. How we appear to the world shouldn't matter to us. What is truly important lies within our conscience. In spite of the misery in this life, some things are eternal and cannot be erased, like my memories of you, which will accompany me to my grave.

Yours always,
Fidel

November 16, 1953

My Dearest Fidel,

With great happiness and pleasure, I read your letter and read it again. Don't think for a moment that it was necessary to reassure me about your feelings. . . . I'm your friend and I never forget about you. You know that. . . .

I've started writing to you so many times. I can't find an excuse for my silence, but I know you understand me and will always indulge me. . . . I am currently absorbed by [the novel] *Jean Christophe*. I love it. I was going to send it to you. Speaking of literature, do you really enjoy French writers? I haven't read them except for Rolland, but I believe that no writer except Proust has a greater sensibility and capacity for observation. . . .

I've had three weeks of rest because my boss is on a trip to the States. What a surprise it was to hear from you. I never imagined that you knew where I worked. . . . I read often, listen to music, and even paint a little. If one day I paint something halfway presentable, I'll send it to you. . . . I spend all of my free time at home. I've never liked going shopping, because I spend too much, and I don't like playing checkers. But I'm absorbed by television. Even if a program is terrible, I watch the whole thing, hoping that the next one will be better. Before I know it, it's eleven or twelve o'clock and I lie down on the bed to read. . . .

My doctor [Naty's husband, Orlando Fernández] is well and working all the time. He's exhausted; the poor man. He works at his medicine, reads, talks, thinks about it. That's why he's so successful. The other day I asked him if he wanted to play some cards or do a puzzle and he replied: "What for?" He'd rather use the time to read a good science text. And, after all, he's right. Much as I insist that once in a while he concentrate on something other than his profession, there isn't a hope. . . . Please write whenever you can. I'm grateful to you for having broken the ice. . . . Don't hesitate to ask me for anything. Until next time and may God be with you.

As always,
Natty

On a Saturday evening in early January, when the brilliant trumpet vine is still in bloom, Naty Revuelta is waiting for me at the entrance to her house in Havana. Some nights, the street lamp on the corner is burning, but not tonight. I can barely see her outline, hardly make out that she's there, that she's standing at the top of the winding stairs which lead to her front door.

It isn't always like this, but tonight an uncomfortable darkness spreads over her neighborhood. To conserve scarce fuel, there are electric-power cuts every evening in some part of the city. Tonight, there are lights in the center of town, but not in the Nuevo Vedado, not on the wide, silent street where Naty lives.

As Naty's mother, Doña Natica, has often said, on this sort of night the Nuevo Vedado is as black as the inside of a cat. Fear surrounds this time of black cats and flickering candles. For a moment, standing on the street outside Naty's house, about to climb the twisting stairs, I can't see at all. I'm alone, frightened, and unsure of my footing. And, of course, I haven't brought a flashlight with me. Imagine playing a game of blindman's buff, but with strangers, and outside the familiar boundaries of a childhood garden.

It was a revelation to me when I first arrived. Each night, Fidel Castro plunges another neighborhood into darkness. Why do I make it so personal? Sometimes I imagine Fidel at a child's

Monopoly board, with a strange, sinister smile on his face. The streets are all in Havana—Línea, Calzada, la Calle 23, Obispo, O'Reilly—and he is deciding which parts of the city he'll black out. But he won't touch his valuable hotels, not ever: Baltic Avenue or Marvin Gardens, but not the Hotel Riviera, or the Hotel Nacional.

Whenever darkness comes—the lights go out a few times a week in each neighborhood—a general anxiety permeates the air. A friend of mine gets into his car and drives as far as he can until he comes to a part of the city that hasn't had a power cut. Often he sits at the wheel for three or four hours at a time, beneath the dim light of the street lamp. Does he feel as safe as he did as a small child, when he insisted that the light in his room not be turned out at night? Another friend takes sleeping pills and crawls into bed; oblivion, too, is a form of deliverance.

Some people don't mind the imposed, official night at all; the enveloping blackness can be a great blessing. After all, if you want to hide from reality, pretend you're someone else, the night is more than useful. At night, without lights, it's easier, for example, to hide a suckling pig from the local authorities. Across the street from Naty's house, I can hear the creature's grunts punctuating the night air.

Tomorrow, a prominent surgeon will remove the pig's vocal cords so that the authorities don't hear him and he doesn't get everyone into trouble. For health reasons, it's illegal to have a pig in your bathtub and, arguably, it's immoral for a surgeon to waste his time operating on an animal's throat. But the surgeon—a man whose Chinese bicycle was stolen last month—hasn't the transportation to get to the hospital where he can practice medicine. Young, energetic, a man who needs to exercise his considerable talents, he's as enthusiastic about performing the unusual surgery as his family seems to be about the prospective *lechón asado*. Fidel Castro may have canceled Christmas, but not the urge to celebrate it by roasting a suckling pig.

Because I'm an American, I'm living at a clean, well-lighted hotel; for foreigners, there are no enforced black nights. Leaving the hotel behind me, I've come to this darkened, candlelit house to see the letters that Naty Revuelta and Fidel Castro wrote to each other. He sent the first on November 7, 1953, when he was in a prison on the Isle of Pines, serving a sentence for his raid on a Batista garrison; his correspondent was a restless married woman living with her family in Havana.

Naty first met Fidel in November 1952. The night was moonlit, and Naty was standing on the steps of the famous *escalinata*, the wide stone staircase that leads to the entrance of the University of Havana. It was the anniversary of the 1871 assassination by the Spanish military of a group of medical students from the university. "A young man who was training with Fidel introduced us to each other. I remember that the meeting was brief, uneventful: 'Fidel, you wanted to meet Naty.' That's all. But then, one evening, shortly after we had met, the same young man came to me and said: 'Fidel wants to know if he can come to visit you.' I said, 'Of course. After five o'clock, I'm always home.'"

For almost two years, beginning in November 1953, Naty Revuelta and Fidel Castro exchanged their thoughts on philosophy, religion, literature. After a while, their letters make it clear that the rebel leader and the housewife were immensely involved in each other. She must know the books that he's reading. Does he like Romain Rolland, Marcel Proust? He's afraid that he's not worthy of her: "Swear that my letters don't bore you." The irony of having to read the letters between them by candlelight isn't lost on either Naty or me.

A SHAFT of light falls upon Naty from an elegant ivory taper she holds in front of her. In the glow, I can see the skeleton of the house that is both a sanctuary and a prison. As she closes the grilled, iron-barred door behind us, she turns the heavy key in the lock, turns it again, and again. "There are so many robberies," she says, "it's not like before. I worry that someone will come in and steal me blind."

Naty Revuelta reveals herself in a charming, dated English. It's the idiom she learned in the 1940s, when she went to prep school in Philadelphia and to Marjorie Webster, a business college in Washington, D.C. "Hellzapoppin," for example, is her favorite response when something dramatic has happened.

Naty Revuelta in the candlelight, so elegant, in a white dress—its bold jet buttons from a silk-faille jacket of her mother's, a gray chiffon scarf around her shoulders—doesn't look as though she belongs in Havana. Not in today's Havana, anyway. She reminds me of another time, of the era of sophisticated film heroines like Rita Hayworth, Yvonne De Carlo, Dolores Del Rio—the women who wore furs around their throats, and diamonds in their upswept hair, and danced with handsome men in the grill rooms of fashionable supper clubs.

Postwar Havana, like Paris and Buenos Aires in the twenties and thirties, was an enchanted place: King Leopold of Belgium at the golf course with the Count of Barcelona; the Duchess of Alba at the Gómez-Menas' ball; the black-tie dinners after the regatta at the Havana Yacht Club, where the winner of the Copa Bacardí sat on a high leather chair singing "Lobo de Mar," with Carole Lombard in the chorus. It was no accident that El Encanto (The Enchantment) was the name of the leading department store.

What has Naty to do with Havana now, an unglamorous

Third World city? At La Floridita, where Ernest Hemingway held court, there are grease stains on the tablecloths, and an indifferent waiter serves canned fruit to tourists wearing Lycra running shorts. What resident of Havana has 120 pesos, half a month's salary, for a bottle of rum?

In Havana, the aging *jineteras*—the prostitutes of twenty-three and twenty-four—have started to complain that it's hard for them to compete with the thirteen-year-old "virgins" who walk along the same sweeping Malecón. The glamorous women, those who resembled Naty Revuelta, have gone from the city forever, taking with them their ermine wraps and their dancing pumps.

A portrait of Naty Revuelta dominates the entrance hall in her house. A beautiful young woman stares out from the heavily painted, white background of the canvas. She wears a green evening dress that calls attention to her graceful shoulders. The prominent cardiologist Orlando Fernández Ferrer had commissioned this portrait of Naty, his stunning bride—a woman young enough to be his daughter. Her haughtiness seems to communicate not arrogance so much as emptiness. She seems to have no thoughts, no memories. It's as though her roots were cinematic, celluloid. Didn't Felix de Cossío, Havana society's favorite portrait painter, understand that there was something strong beneath the surface?

Did Fidel write to Naty because he relished winning the heart of one of the hated bourgeoisie? The woman in the portrait would have seemed quite conventional to Fidel. Doesn't she convey as much in the first letter she writes to him on the Isle of Pines? ("I've never liked going shopping, because I spend too much, and I don't like playing checkers.")

Wasn't she just another beautiful woman who found herself bored with her distracted, much older husband? ("My doctor [Orlando] is well and working all the time. . . . The other day I asked him if he wanted to play some cards or do a puzzle and he replied: 'What for?'") And yet not so. For Naty at least, more than a dalliance was developing: for her, it would be a lifelong devotion.

Naty Revuelta Clews, now more than seventy years old, retains the authority of her considerable beauty. Tonight, as we sit down on the terrace to talk about the book, she fastens me with her startling green eyes; and she purses the provocative, sensuous mouth. Fashionable, tanned rather than fair, wearing white silk, her feet encased in black-and-white spectator pumps, Naty throws her head back in laughter, recovering her freshness.

In some people, there is no resistance to time. The progress from childhood to old age is gentle, uncomplicated. My grand-mother embraced age as though she'd waited for it all her life. I would look at a photograph of her when she was twenty, and it seemed that the young woman in the image had vanished without a trace. It's as though she'd always wanted to take flight, to move as far as she could from the time of her life when she had lost her father's protection and faced, for the first time, her hus-band's indifference.

Naty Revuelta resists time. She tries to bend it around, sending it spinning in the direction of the past. Because the pres-ent is so bleak, so inhospitable, she tolerates it—the woman, after all, is a survivor—but at great cost. "Some things are eter-nal and cannot be erased, like my memories of you, which will accompany me to my grave," Fidel wrote to her. Whatever those memories may be to Fidel today, for Naty they remain vivid; it is in them that she lives most intensely.

Why would she permit me—indeed encourage me—to tell her story? Memories are what she has to hurl against the bitter experiences of the last three decades—a span in which she has lost not only Fidel but both of her daughters. In those dreadful

Felix de Cossío's portrait of Naty

years—as her mother, Doña Natica, never ceases to remind her—the early promise of the revolution has come to nothing.

But memories aren't organized; they lack sequence. They can't fulfill Naty's desire to give a permanent reality to her romance with Fidel. Writing down her story, giving it a coherence in time, has to be the answer. Possibly she's chosen me to write it because she believes I'll accept her version of what happened. After all, I wasn't there, never met the cast of characters. It is a time of expectations—for both of us.

AT NIGHT, it's easier for Naty to live; she welcomes the camouflage, the disguise, and, above all, the silence. When there is no light, Naty spends the evenings at home, chain-smoking and drinking strong black coffee. In the largest bedroom in the house, her mother sleeps soundly: "I couldn't even have a conversation with you if my mother were around," she tells me. "She doesn't leave me alone for a minute. And she blames me for everything that's happened in Cuba."

Naty has taken care of her mother for several years. Without some ambivalence, and more than a hint of resentment at the elderly woman's manipulations, it would have been impossible for her to do this. Sometimes the elderly forget that, for others, the present maintains its attractions. So they try to suck you into their past; they dispose of your own reality. Suspended in her mother's force field, Naty fights the feeling that she's a butterfly pinned to the walls of the dim house.

Distancing herself from Doña Natica, Naty confesses her admiration for passionate women in literature: Anna Karenina, for one, who left her dutiful husband for the dashing Count Vronsky. "Fortunately," she says, "my mother doesn't read Russian novels." Naty Revuelta can only imagine what Doña Natica would have said of Anna, particularly at the end of the novel, when she throws herself in front of a moving train. Doña Natica, she's certain, would have seen it coming.

When we sit together on her terrace—we can see only each other in the candlelight—Naty takes out the letters that are so sacred to her. She removes the blue silken ribbon from the packet. She does this slowly, silently; it is the beginning of a ritual she has performed so often, for so many people. She has brought the letters from a hiding place in her bedroom— underneath her cache of pale silk stockings—where she has carefully harbored them, counting them, rereading them aloud to herself.

As Naty holds the first letter in her hand, her expression changes. Imagine. It is 1953. Naty Revuelta writes to Fidel Castro from home or from her office. Fidel writes to Naty from his prison cell. Lingering over his words, pausing to remember the moment, she wrestles with never-forgotten dreams, struggles as though time hadn't gone about its dreadful mission, transforming her desire for Fidel into painful memories of the past.

Fidel's handwriting is small and cramped, but deliberately so. (A prisoner's letters could be only a page long. Later, the prison censor would befriend them both and permit him more paper. Everything seemed possible then, absolutely everything.) She usually types her letters to him. She does this on an old Smith-Corona, after hours, from her desk at Esso Standard Oil. The world created in the letters has a strange purity, an insularity, that pushes back the conflicts and disguises, the natural oppositions that would surface later and drive the lovers far apart from each other.

Perhaps for all of us there is a single moment, one from which everything else in life follows, and without which experiences make little sense, even to ourselves. For years after Fidel came to power, after her husband and older daughter had left her, Naty would read to her friends from the letters. "Poor

Naty," someone said to me. "The light went out for her too soon." She couldn't re-create the world of the letters, or find another in which she could breathe. Her story, she would argue—and most people who know her would agree—must have, as its very center, this moment with Fidel.

Isle of Pines
November 24, 1953

Dear Natty,

Your letter has given me great pleasure. So many memories have come back to me. . . .

Of course I like French literature very much. . . . Reading *Jean Christophe,* I feel just as I did when I read Victor Hugo's *Les Miserables*; I hoped it would never end. The novels belong to different eras and it's only natural that we are more enthusiastic about the work of Rolland. He's our contemporary and, in his writings, has defended the greatest social causes of this century. . . .

I'll be waiting to receive the painting that you've offered me. It must be very valuable, as is everything that you create. As for my son, I haven't seen him this month, nor will I be able to see him in the next. I often think of him. . . . I only want you to send me three single-spaced sheets of writing, containing all the grace and charm that is always present in your letters.

Lots of kisses for [Nina, Naty's daughter] and for her mother lots of affection.

Fidel

Naty Revuelta is still looking through me at herself, in 1953, when she was twenty-eight and shared a house with her husband, Orlando, and their daughter, Nina. Fidel, the illegitimate son of a servant his father, Ángel Castro, later married, had a more tenuous social presence. Mirta Díaz-Balart, Fidel's lawful wife, the mother of his only legitimate son, hadn't Naty's sophistication. A simple girl from the provinces, she had no intellectual pursuits, nor was she interested in revolutionary politics. But she was well connected, and while her husband was in prison, she would profit from her family's ties to General Batista.

Peter Bourne, in his biography of Fidel Castro, writes about the trauma of the Cuban leader's birth and suggests that it was responsible for his insatiable need for public glorification. "A soap opera was broadcast on the radio about a fictional family in the village of Biran that bore sufficient resemblance to the Castro family. . . . In it, a point was made of describing the children's illegitimacy. The public revelation, just as he was entering adolescence, of this fact, even if it was already known to many of his peers as well as the priests, must have been an excruciating and humiliating experience that must have left an emotional scar."

Illiterate, though he was a rich man, Ángel Castro had a humble background that made Fidel a pariah in Naty's circles. Certainly not a *criollo*, the elder Castro was a poor Galician immigrant turned confidence man. A strong, crude soldier in the Spanish cavalry, he came to the island in the 1890s, worked for United Fruit, and acquired more wealth for himself than the company auditors might have thought proper. By the time of his death in 1956, his sugar plantation employed more than five hundred men and spread over ten thousand acres.

But Fidel's intelligence was enormous and so, too, his fascination with power. At Belén, the famous Jesuit school that trained his mind and formed his sensibility, he played at baseball but studied law. When he graduated, the yearbook said:

"We are sure that, after his law studies, he will make a brilliant name for himself. Fidel has what it takes. . . ."

Sentenced to fifteen years in prison for leading an attack on the military garrison at Moncada, Fidel braced himself for a very long separation from his family. More important, he postponed his plan to overthrow General Batista's regime. From a prison cell—a place where his energies were contained, turned inward, and where he had nothing to do—he read, studied, and wrote. He composed letters to Naty Revuelta, a beautiful woman who was falling in love with the revolution, and, of course, with him.

NOTHING fills Naty with more pleasure than the thought of reading the letters aloud. She loves to see her audience startled. Is this really Fidel? Preferring that I not read the letters alone, she argues that they won't make sense without her interpretation. Perhaps her intonation isn't perfect, she insists, but its accents convey the right meaning. Is she protecting herself, responding to past humiliation? I wonder whether she has shown the letters—on an evening, for example, when everyone had had too much rum—to someone who read them aloud with sarcasm, mocking Fidel's sentiments.

In the flickering light—the tropical night air threatens to blow out the candle—I can hear Naty clearing her throat. With each letter she reads, the tone of her voice will become more seductive: "Can you see why this was the man I loved?" His enemies, she agrees, would insist that Fidel was a master manipulator—a man who pretended to be an ideal courtier because it suited him. Perhaps he hoped for Naty's financial backing or, as suggested before, wanted to win her to get back at Havana's elite.

Naty's thought is different. She draws the picture of a

romance that grew out of an *amistad amorosa* (a loving friendship)—one where the cement is mutual support. "I responded," he writes to her at one point, "to the most generous friendship in my life. . . ." She answers: "Your letters to me provide nourishment for my soul . . . help me to know my feelings . . . and to calm my fears." In my own perception, Naty sought spiritual transcendence in Fidel quite as much as sexual excitement. Not everyone agrees. There is a resistance to seeing Naty as a complicated woman who was, and perhaps is now, imprisoned in a biography too compressed to contain her.

Havana
November 27, 1953

Dear Fidel,

How wonderful to hear from you again! . . .

You tell me of the pleasure you get from my letters and that it's an unimaginable privilege for a prisoner, but aren't we all prisoners, Fidel? If absolute freedom existed, wouldn't I be there visiting you, embracing you. . . ? But I can't. After all, I'm not free to do as I wish and this, in and of itself, is a sentence which I must serve. . . .

You flatter me! You flatter me! . . . Fidel, deep down inside, I'm desperate because I still have much to learn. . . . I know a little about many things as opposed to a great deal about one thing. Sometimes I feel lost in this vast abyss which ignorance creates, because I know how life ought to be and what people should know in order to give meaning to their lives, and I am unhappy with myself.

I don't consider myself a failure, because I still have many years ahead of me. But I'd like to be more than I am and good at whatever I become, or, if that's not possible, I'd like to know how to adapt to the environment and how to rid myself of an anxiety of the spirit that prohibits me from enjoying what I already have. I live in a perpetual state of confusion. I try to do so much that, in the long run, I don't get anything accomplished. . . .

Can you help me? Put my thoughts in order. . . . ?

Always,
Natty

In 1953, a young Cuban socialite discovers that she has it in her to have a more meaningful life. Can one embrace this idea? Certainly, she has picked a time when women of her class—those who live in Havana—are continuing to devote themselves almost entirely to being decorative. But Naty Revuelta is no longer satisfied with winning her matches at the Vedado Tennis Club, no longer content to sit at home in the evenings watching television, waiting for her husband to return from his work at the clinic.

On that first evening, Naty read to me for more than an hour. What Felix de Cossío hadn't seen in Naty's face when he painted her portrait surfaced in her letters: the seriousness; the sense of adventure; the curiosity about ideas; the desire for release into a more passionate existence. "In a sense," she confided in me, "what happened to me, the falling in love with Fidel, was the experience of my entire generation. Remember his triumphant arrival in Havana, the crowds cheering? Weren't most of us in love with Fidel?"

WITHOUT warning, the lights come back on. Then Doña Natica enters the room and the mood shifts. She asks Naty to bring out her English grandfather's tea service: delicate flowers of celadon green decorate the fragile cups and saucers. To get them, Naty has to climb a ladder in the pantry, find the teapot in the back of the closet, and bring it down into the kitchen, where she prepares her mother's favorite tea. "Once my mother had five servants," Naty says; "now she has only me." A calm descends on Doña Natica, as though the cinnamon tea, perhaps the teacups themselves, had magical properties.

Naty is wearing a brooch that Wilfredo Lam, the famous Cuban artist, once created for her—an abstract design on paper that he had placed in a tiny oval frame. (Doña Natica never met Wilfredo Lam; when she had the chance, she dismissed him as unpresentable: *"un negro, medio chino."*)

From a suede pouch that she's brought into the room with her, Doña Natica removes her own treasures: the Art Deco diamond-and-sapphire clip from Tiffany's; the emerald earrings that her brother Bebo brought from South America; the gold Victorian locket that belonged to her grandmother Selina Alcock Clews.

A strange transaction? Doña Natica has brought out her jewelry because, for a moment, she has an audience to appreciate it. Before her world shattered, having diamonds, emeralds, and sapphires made a difference. It no longer does, but the precious stones remain crucial to Doña Natica's identity. If I'm going to write about her, she has to show me the jewelry: it will tell me who she is.

She hovers over each piece; a Swiss merchant looking through his ancient jeweler's loupe couldn't wear a more serious expression. After telling me about the value of each stone, she returns the pieces one by one to the suede pouch. Before the revolution, women wore their furs, their jewels. Now there's no such thing as a formal evening, or a dance at the country club.

The Cuba of Doña Natica and her daughter is over. The artifacts that remain are suited for a museum: the precious stones, the bundle of letters. To Naty Revuelta, Fidel had come in a whirlwind, and then he'd gone from her forever. The romance has cost her so much. "But," she says, "I have no regrets." She rises from her chair and walks towards her bedroom, where she hides the letters in the blue satin case that bears her monogram. "I have no regrets at all."

CHAPTER 3

Doña Natica

MANY years ago, when General Fulgencio Batista ruled the island of Cuba, Doña Natica attended a dinner in honor of a foreign prince. As she curtsied in her long evening dress—black silk chiffon, against which her emerald earrings flashed—the prince was heard to mutter that he had never seen a more attractive woman. But that came as no surprise to Doña Natica, whose English father had told her often that she was beautiful. *"Mi rosa de oro* [My golden rose]," he used to say when he carried her in his arms, into his magic circle.

Doña Natica, suspended in time, impervious to change, concentrates on her favorite subject: the glorious past. With her fine bones and clear blue eyes, this elegant woman, now almost a hundred years old, might be a figure in an eighteenth-century English painting: imperious, haughty, aristocratic. Tropical colors seem too strong for her, the aromas too pungent. She is an evocation of the island's past, a colonial grafting onto the native plant.

Since a bad fall a number of years ago, Doña Natica has been confined to Naty's house. Every morning, when she awakens, she circles her bedroom and stares at the sacred relics of her past: the silver brushes with their swirling monograms, the hand-painted fans edged in white lace, the crystal bottles of Guerlain perfumes. She lingers at the portrait of her daughter, Naty, on her wedding day. "She had everything, a husband who adored her, two beautiful daughters, five household servants, twelve goblets of Baccarat crystal. . . ."

On her daily round, Doña Natica visits Margarita, a porcelain doll dressed in white muslin. When she was very small, Doña Natica's brother borrowed his mother's scissors and snipped off all of Margarita's golden curls. He promised his sister that they would grow back, condemning the doll and Natica to a long, hopeless vigil. Another betrayal.

Doña Natica's memories come in waves, flinging her backwards and forwards across the century. Sometimes, she remembers the sedate Havana of her childhood—the Café Doménica, where she sipped an orange *granizado* and her father wore a Panama hat. She sits in cafés that serve minute cakes of chocolate, citron, and almond paste. Along O'Reilly Street, she shops for Spanish shawls, for tortoiseshell combs and embroidery from the Canary Islands. It was enchanting then, wasn't it—in the sunlight, under royal palms and Indian-laurel trees?

At other times, the elderly woman's thoughts turn to the irreverent, pleasure-loving Havana of the twenties. In the bar of the Hotel Plaza, she remembers meeting a distinguished gentleman with a Bombay foulard around his neck and a sprig of orange blossom in his buttonhole. He might have been her father's friend. At the Hotel Inglaterra, Doña Natica joins her friends in the surreal dining room decorated with the imagined arms of Pontius Pilate.

She remembers driving home late at night, the car tracing the graceful curve of the Malecón, the wide seawall that embraces the harbor. At night, with its crescent of street lights forming a glittering band of diamonds, the Malecón becomes an image of Doña Natica's beloved Havana. In that moment, the past overwhelms the present, finally defeating it, and Doña Natica is at peace.

NATY'S gray stone house—a grim fortress set high above the street—looms over its paint-peeled, forlorn neighbors. At the doorbell's ring, there are familiar sounds: Doña Natica's high-pitched voice, the frantic barking of her granddaughter's white terrier, Naty's keys turning in the locks. In rooms crammed with furniture, silver, and crystal, Doña Natica presides over the past. It's as if Miss Havisham in *Great Expectations* had not only stopped the clock at the moment of her greatest disappointment but had moved herself into the sealed room to guard the crumbling wedding dress, the piece of moldy cake.

Because I've lived with my grandmother, I'm comfortable with proud, strong women of a certain age. To survive as a child, I learned to listen to my grandmother's favorite stories: how her great-uncle had had, then had lost the privilege of wearing his hat in front of the King of Spain; how her cousin Aurelia's harp teacher had mysteriously vanished into the night; how the elaborate fountain in Havana had come to be called *el bidet de Paulina Alsina*. Within these anecdotes (although I didn't know it then) was the master tale of my grandmother's life.

Doña Natica's biography, I was certain, could be recovered by reconstructing her experience as her father's "golden rose." But whenever I asked a question—What is your earliest memory of your mother? Did you ever go to the beach?—she answered me with little more than a charming smile. Often, she'd put it like this: *"En boca cerrada, no entran moscas."* ("Flies never get into a mouth when it's closed.")

She never feared me. Rather, she welcomed the attention. To an elderly woman, being written about is a sign of her importance. Furthermore, Doña Natica was preparing for death—a time when many people want to tell their story. Her expectations were that I would write what she told me and nothing more. Her behavior, her desire to influence my narrative, was the other side of her pride.

For Doña Natica, the matter at hand was making herself into an aristocrat. She was doing what the very old do when visiting the past, cleaning, reconstructing. Her withdrawals were calculated, intended to erase that part of her history which was less than noble. She counted upon my collusion. I never contradicted her; but I didn't agree with her either. It didn't seem to me that I had to please her by attributing aristocratic characteristics to her and avoiding the evidence that had set her down among the middle classes eating *arroz con pollo* and worrying about paying her daughter's school tuition.

What Doña Natica wants to talk about is the Queen of England. With a wave of her blue-veined hand, she holds up a recent photograph of Elizabeth II in *Hola* (the Spanish magazine) and asks, quite seriously, if I see her own strong resemblance to the Queen. She's very fond of the English monarch, who still wears white kid gloves and feeds her favorite corgis from matching silver bowls. For Doña Natica, the similarities between herself and the Queen are startling: Both had English fathers who adored them and difficult husbands. More to the point, the two women both wrestle with impossible children determined to drive them to their ruin. Diana, Princess of Wales, separated from Charles because he wouldn't leave his mistress, Camilla Parker Bowles. How different is Doña Natica's own family? Naty, enthroned in the marriage of her mother's dreams, risked her husband for love of Fidel Castro.

Whenever someone enters the house, Doña Natica, under her breath, makes a comment about the color of the person's skin. Never leaving the house, she lives in a lily-white Cuba that exists in particular enclaves of Miami, not Havana. At night, she prays that her granddaughter will marry a white man. Talking about Afro-Cubans: *"Fidel les cortó las colas,"* she says, *"y los bajó de los árboles."* ("Fidel cut off their tails and brought them down from the trees.")

Doña Natica holds Elizabeth II's portrait up to the mirror; she sees her own reflection next to that of the monarch. She remembers the young Princess Elizabeth returning to London from Kenya, where she had learned of her father's death. Everything had changed while the princess slept at Treetops and listened to the "kra kra kra" of monkeys outside her window. When her own father died, Doña Natica ceased to be a princess, but, unlike Elizabeth, she never became the Queen.

HERBERT CLEWS—the man who would never be king— first arrived in Havana at the end of the last century. Born in 1864, in the English mining town of Newcastle-under-Lyme, Herbert entered the world in the generation after the industrial revolution had changed the face of his own country: locomotives pushed through the dense green woodlands; the ancient coupling of wind and sail gave way to the miracle of steam. If a young man wanted to secure his future in Cuba, he would go there not to search for pots of gold but, through the power of machines, to turn the island's sugar into gold.

The provincial Herbert Clews wouldn't have made a connection between the grand schemes of the Spanish conquistadors and his own measured desire for adventure. Still, there were similarities, points of connection. Ever since Columbus's voyage, ambitious young men, evading the narrow fate that awaited them at home, had bailed out of small towns in Europe and headed across the ocean to the Americas.

Growing up in his parents' severe Methodist household,

Herbert felt claustrophobic. His parents, Ralph and Selina Clews, must have found their son's restlessness troubling, an indication of a possible nervous disorder or, worse yet, a sign of a self-indulgent nature. The Clewses had modest expectations for Herbert. They looked forward to his settling down to manage the small family coal mine. In Newcastle-under-Lyme, they reasoned, he would become a man of substance; the village would take its communal measure from the cut of his frock coat.

A Midlands Cassandra might have predicted that Herbert would leave his homeland. She would have guessed how much he hated Newcastle-under-Lyme: the black nights which shrouded the gray winter days; the grim countenance of the village minister; the silences of a father who never smiled and coughed incessantly. At school, during the tedious classes, the boring recitations, Herbert found it difficult to be attentive. But the time would come when he could leave; he must have dreamed about that.

Shortly before he died, Herbert had reconstructed his memories in stories, transforming a somber childhood into a marvelous preamble to his voyage to the Americas. He recalled the fabulous globe that the teacher had positioned in the corner of the schoolroom. It had a particular attraction for Herbert, serving as a mariner's chart, giving direction to his imaginative flights. He savored the pleasures of leaving England behind and traveling to the brightly colored landscape of Cuba.

Herbert Clews eventually came to Cuba as a trained engineer, on behalf of Fawcett, Preston and Co., suppliers of technology to the sugar mills. He wouldn't remain in their employ for long, but modesty, restraint, simplicity of ambitions would govern his future. I think of T. S. Eliot's lines: "No! I am not Prince Hamlet, nor was meant to be; /Am an attendant lord, one that will do / To swell a progress, start a scene or two."

By the time Herbert arrived in Cuba, large sugar plantations dominated the island; their owners had a touch of the robber baron about them, ruling the vast estates that sustained a majority of the island's people. (The greatest of the later, twentieth-century, *latifundistas* [landowners], Julio Lobo, was rumored to have had a fling with Doña Natica. When asked about it, she repeats her line: *"En boca cerrada, no entran moscas."*)

In 1894, when Herbert Clews arrived in Cuba, he hadn't heard of Soledad, nor did he care about the sugar business. His excitement was in the contrasts between Cuba and Newcastle-under-Lyme. To begin with, the island seemed so exotic, shaped like a bird's tongue or a Turkish scimitar. More to the point, the passionate struggle for Cuba's freedom was imminent. For a young man, nothing was more appealing than this noble fight for independence from Spain.

In the aristocratic quarter, the colonial families continued to live as though the future would never touch them. They hosted family theatricals in the evenings, celebrated the carnival season with their children, and bought their pastries at the confectioners' on Lombillo Street. Walking along the narrow streets, Spanish soldiers in seersucker uniforms and straw hats with red cockades fostered this illusion of an unchanging world.

But the story of Spain's dominion over Cuba, an adventure that had lasted almost four hundred years, was coming to an end. By the time Herbert arrived in the province of Pinar del Río, prepared to sell his machines to the sugar plantations, his heart belonged to the revolutionaries. In no time at all, he was smuggling rifles and ammunition to the insurgents.

When the Spanish shelled his storehouse, the Englishman joined the Cristóbal Colón Brigade and became a captain in the rebel forces. Wounded in battle, Herbert Clews, now proclaimed a Cuban hero, retired from the army with the rank of colonel. The Spanish-American War had served his interests, offering him a chance to sow his wild oats and liberating him from the dreariness of selling machines for Fawcett, Preston. Without the war, he might have become another tired middle-aged salesman traveling back and forth across the island, a brown moth circling round a dim light.

HERBERT CLEWS' naïveté, the ignorance of his revolutionary zeal, didn't affect his life adversely. In the hurricane's eye, it's not uncommon to experience calm and, often, a very blue sky. But far from Herbert's battlefield, at the storm's outer edges, the destruction of the infant republic was taking place. Cuba hadn't won her freedom; at best, she had changed owners.

At 9:40 p.m. on February 15, 1898, the noise of the explosion was deafening. The *Maine*—a U.S. battleship moored in Havana—blew up in the harbor, fatally wounding some 288 American sailors—"bluejackets," they were called. That the American consul in Havana had been eager for the protection of the *Maine* came as no surprise. The bitter war between Spain and Cuba (a fight for independence that had been going on since 1895) worsened by the moment, threatening everyone's safety. But there was another, more subtle reason. A U.S. military presence in Havana hinted at America's intention to defeat Spain and take over the valuable sugar island.

Encouraged by William Randolph Hearst's newspapers, the Americans blamed Spain for the *Maine*. ("Remember the *Maine*. To hell with Spain.") Having found a rationale for entering the war, the United States fought enthusiastically on the side of the Cubans. But long before a fierce Teddy Roosevelt climbed to the top of San Juan Hill, those who understood power knew that independence would elude the Cubans.

Spain's "ever-faithful" isle was to become a playing field for the American businessman. Ask Edwin Atkins who owned Cuba.

At the Spanish surrender, the authorities raised the American flag, not the Cuban. When Spain and the United States signed the treaty ending the war, the Cubans weren't even invited to the ceremony. With the imposition of the Platt Amendment, giving the American government the right to intervene in the island's affairs, Cuba became a foster child of the United States—an abused minor who could be taken to task at whim. The Americans, those "buffaloes with silver teeth," would create a resentment among the territorial Cubans that would last until Fidel Castro converted popular discontent into active enthusiasm for his revolution.

When the war ended, Herbert joined Havana's municipal police force. While settling a fight in front of her house, he met his future wife, Natalia Álvarez de la Ballina—a blushing girl of provincial origins who immediately stole his heart. No longer the naïve revolutionary, Herbert was a dignified authoritarian figure in a police uniform when he married Señorita Álvarez, and this was Doña Natica's image of him as a father. It was a good marriage. Together, Herbert and Natalia, settling into the Cuban middle class, prepared for the pleasure, the excitement of their new adventure.

Herbert Clews, once a young idealist, became a comfortable conservative—a man who would have no problems living on an island dominated by the imperial Americans. His investments in Cuba, made with partners from the United States, would stake his family to the respectable, bourgeois existence he most wanted for them. His intention wasn't to ride the high waves but to cause, at most, a slight swell in the waters. (Herbert's most ambitious scheme, perhaps, would be his investment in the Cuban Land Company, which envisioned creating a model American city on a hundred thousand acres forty miles west of Havana.)

The swift transformation from blood-red radical to self-satisfied conservative must have distanced his former friends, but Herbert was comfortable as he moved into the middle of the increasingly American-influenced establishment. He wasn't constricted by his lack of family money and breeding. As an Englishman, and a white man in the Caribbean, Herbert could climb the social ladder—a movement that would have been denied him in the country of his birth. Herbert would never sabotage that position. *Antes era incendiero,* the Cubans say, *ahora soy bombero.* (Once I was an arsonist, but now I'm a fireman.)

Naty doesn't see it like that. Defending her fateful attraction to Fidel Castro, she proposes a clear, philosophical line of descent from her English grandfather—the ancestor who she believes accounts for her own bold spirit—to the Cuban guerrilla who fought for independence because he believed in freedom. Naty imagines Herbert Clews in the mountains—a splendid rider, a careful shot, cutting his way through the long grass with his machete—bravely facing the opposing infantry and a shower of Mauser bullets. And she sees Fidel Castro as his spiritual heir—a man of honor, holding out in the Sierra Maestra, fighting against the tyranny of General Batista.

But for Doña Natica, Herbert Clews stands as a proud, protective figure who would have disdained Fidel Castro and seen to it that his daughter remained in the magic garden forever. Doña Natica, with her delusions about royalty, sometimes thinks of her parents as Nicholas and Alexandra. She loves the story of the Russian Czar's attempts to shield his daughters as the Communist assassins peppered them with bullets that bounced off the diamonds hidden inside their corsets. She can see Fidel Castro only as the snake in the Eden of her childhood and herself as her father's flower, reluctantly transplanted from his spring garden into Fidel Castro's nightmare world of brambles and tangled weeds.

Later, in New York, burrowing into library archives, I found an account of Doña Natica's spiritual female ancestors: the *rosas de oro* gilded long before her birth. Granted, Doña Natica was born at the turn of the century, when Queen Victoria's days were numbered, but, still, in Havana, pampered white women lived as though under a house arrest imposed a hundred years before.

Doña María de las Mercedes Beltrán de Santa Cruz, the Countess of Merlín—a Cuban aristocrat living in Paris, who revisited Havana in 1840—was witness to the housebound existence of the likes of a nineteenth-century Doña Natica. Writing to her friend George Sand, the countess elaborated on the idle schedule of a protected Havana woman. During the day, she never left her house. She might while away the hours making clothes for the servants and the children, but for the most part, since the heat was intolerable, she spent the day in the bath, eating fruit, or rocking in a chair. At the end of the afternoon, she would climb into her *volanta* (a large-wheeled one-horse carriage), driven by a *calesero* (a black footman in high boots and silver spurs), to do her shopping. The tradesmen, of course, would bring their wares to her in the carriage. Her feet, encased in satin slippers, never touched the pavement outside her house.

Alejo Carpentier, the Cuban novelist, has said that, until 1925, Havana was a city without women. But from the background, often in whispers, they made themselves heard. Let's not forget the elegant ladies of Havana who had their jewelry melted down to provide aid for George Washington. Money given by these women became the cement on which American independence was erected. When such ladies thought about England, they remembered the humiliating 1762 siege of Havana, which might have set even Doña Natica against the English king.

Now imagine Doña Natica at the time of Fidel's victory. Could she have left the island—a woman nearing sixty, who had never earned her living? Though her experience was different from that described by the Countess of Merlín—even when she was a child, Doña Natica's world was not quite so restrictive—the traditions that governed the lives of women were still observed. Until very recently, most pampered Cuban women, manipulated by husbands and fathers, glided across the historical stage as though in a never-ending celebration of Tchaikovsky's *Sleeping Beauty*.

BORN in 1900, Doña Natica faced her earliest childhood armed with hoops and crinolines. With her parents and her four younger brothers, she lived in the Vedado, the fashionable suburb of Havana—a quiet, charming place that she believed to be a microcosm of the world itself. Soon, the very rich would arrive in the Vedado to build their palaces of stone and marble. But when Doña Natica was a little girl, it was still a simple place where children played in the gardens of the Conde de Pozos Dulces; where cows were brought to private houses so that everyone could taste their sweet, warm milk; where Gypsies entertained the town with dancing bears.

Despite her high, flashing temper, Doña Natica had little of the rebel in her, and none of the restlessness that she would resent in her own daughter, Naty. She accepted the world as a place where a man sought adventure and a woman settled for the protections of a good marriage. From her mother, Natalia, she had inherited an elegant carriage, a lack of intellectual curiosity, and a desire to confine herself to a world of custom

Doña Natica when she was eight

and convention. Natalia Álvarez de la Ballina had never read a poem or listened to a symphony; she rarely left her house.

A traditional Cuban woman, Doña Natica's mother thought it ridiculous for her daughter to be educated, and concentrated instead on cultivating her manners and style. Whenever she could, she took her daughter to Madame Laurent, the seamstress on the Calle O'Reilly; to La Acacia, the jeweler; to the talented milliners the sisters Tapie; and, of course, to Galathea, the fan maker. Proper attention to her English beauty, the thinking surely was, would assure that Doña Natica would marry well, enhance her husband, and produce a brood of children with fair complexions and flaxen curls.

From her father, Herbert Clews, Doña Natica would learn to value respectability and, in return, receive the blessings of their small society. She remembers attending band concerts in the Prado with Herbert, accompanying him to El Clavel, the Chinese florist, where he ordered roses for his wife. During the carnival season, Doña Natica and her brothers masked themselves, decorated the roofs of their house with streamers, and sent confetti and brightly colored streamers into the air. But even then, in the moment when the lord of misrule was in charge, her father chided her if she ran around too much or wrestled with her brothers.

At Las Manacas, a plantation Herbert Clews managed outside the city, there were many trees to climb—the giant ceiba tree held sacred by the ancient Mayans; the mamey, with its delicious pink-orange fruit; the jacaranda, with its fernlike leaves and cool blue blossoms. But Doña Natica's particular favorite was the fountain tree, with its startling fiery blossoms. Her brothers Bebo and Arturo weren't interested in the flowers, or even in the superstition that the fountain tree was a source of witchcraft. They did love to climb it, though, because when they squeezed the unopened buds water gushed forth. The tree became a bouquet of water pistols.

Doña Natica climbed the tree, too—higher than Bebo, who had more fear in him. Nothing frightened her when she was a child; she believed completely in the strength of her body. But once, when she tried to climb the tree by herself, she was caught by her father and sent to her room for doing something dangerous. If she broke her nose, ruined her beauty, who would have her? Herbert Clews, who had escaped from the Midlands, didn't believe that his daughter should climb a tree. Constantly, too, he chided her for fidgeting. "A lady's hands," he would say, "belong in her lap."

Doña Natica's mother would bring her inside and rub cream into her elbows, worrying that, with rough skin and exposure to the sun, Doña Natica would not grow up to be an eligible bride. She would sit her daughter down in the parlor, in front of the iron grille, and lecture her: "A man should support his wife while she remains at home with the servants." But neither of Doña Natica's parents understood that this plan depended for its success on a benevolent world in which a woman could count on her good fortune.

While her brothers read children's editions of Greek myths and of Shakespeare's plays, Doña Natica learned to embroider her initials on a strip of Belgian lace. But she wasn't a curious child and didn't mind most of the restrictions of a young girl's life. Her friend Sara was different, spending hours in her father's library reading Immanuel Kant, even the parts she couldn't understand. Sara had once fallen out of bed while contemplating the immensity of the cosmos.

But the young Doña Natica felt that she absorbed enough history and literature through her father, the man who was to remain her conduit for excitement and romance. Perhaps it was a failure of imagination that she insisted on living in the pages of the storybook world he had created for her. It meant that she brought her destructive delusions with her, her confusion about who she was and what constituted the good life.

I I

MANOLO REVUELTA, with his tender, almost feminine black eyes, was an endearing, sentimental man, who sang songs and played *boleros* on his guitar. Women associated his exotic, olive-skinned good looks with danger, adventure, and romance: Turkish sultans, Arab princes, and Japanese warriors. Doña Natica's beauty was different; when people considered her face, her clear blue eyes, they imagined only English lakes and Devonshire cream. Doña Natica Clews and Manolo Revuelta were drawn to each other because they were beautiful; they existed in the same force field, a handsome *boulevardier* and a young woman who flirted with a black lace fan from the balcony of her father's house.

Manolo's father, Don Agustín Revuelta, a self-made Catalan, had come to Cuba in 1898, entering through the eastern port of Santiago. There he found himself both a bride and a profitable business. A man more practical than political, Don Agustín reacted to the political turmoil of the Spanish-American War with the instincts of a merchant. The army would need cloth for uniforms; the arriving Americans would want to buy fabrics for their tropical wardrobes. He made a fortune selling woolen goods, linen, and cotton to retail stores. When he died in 1915, Don Agustín left a very rich widow and dreamy, artistic children who were not at all interested in selling cloth.

From the time he first met Manolo, Herbert Clews had doubts about his prospective son-in-law. Manolo had come to the house to call on Doña Natica, and Herbert had recognized him. He remembered seeing him at the Hotel Seville, drinking heavily, tearing into the bartender, creating a scene about the bill. When Herbert mentioned the conflict some time later, Manolo insisted that he hadn't been there, that it must have been somebody else. Herbert Clews didn't believe him, and wondered to whom he might be entrusting his finest blossom.

DOÑA NATICA isn't certain, but she believes she met Manolo at a tea dance, given by a friend at the Casino Alemán. He asked her to join him in a "two-step," and, of course, the polonaise. Manolo was a wonderful dancer; some said he was responsible for convincing Chichita Grau del Valle, a leading socialite, that she should surrender her pious opposition to the tango. *Es un baile como otro cualquiera* (It's a dance, no different from any other), chorused the tango's fashionable enthusiasts. After that first party success, Manolo and Natica continued to dance together, winning the "one-step" contest at the *baile blanco* in the Hotel Seville. How could she have resisted him? (It is not lost on Doña Natica that Fidel Castro is probably the only Cuban man who doesn't dance.)

A number of her friends warned Doña Natica not to marry her troubled young man. Juan Pedroso, a childhood confidant, told her that Manolo was weak, a lover of wine and women. Julio Lobo, the sugar baron, who was himself head over heels in love with Doña Natica, also tried to dissuade her from the marriage, suggesting that Manolo was not a reliable man. But Doña Natica wouldn't listen to them or to her father. She insisted that Manolo was a serious man pursuing a degree in the law. In the enchanted garden where she had always lived, everything worked in her favor. Why would she believe that her marriage would be less than a great success?

Doña Natica Clews and Manolo Revuelta were married in

February 1924, at the Capilla del Carmelo in the Vedado. Doña Natica wore a long white lace dress with a train, and walked down the aisle on the arm of her father. The couple's first home, opposite the University of Havana, was so near to the Clews house that the bride visited her parents every morning. Just to reassure himself, Herbert Clews walked past his daughter's house several times each day.

Havana in the twenties was the capital of an island gliding towards a depression—the sugar crisis was about to set in— and reaching out for a leader who promised salvation. At the time of the marriage, General Gerardo Machado was soon to come to power. A descendant of cattle robbers, an ambitious businessman familiar with corruption, and a devotee of the island's fleshpots, Machado nonetheless promised to solve the country's economic crisis, to dedicate himself to reform, and to keep his fingers out of the till. The last promise seemed the most plausible: the general had lost three fingers while working in the country as a butcher.

For nearly four years, General Machado posed as a successful patriot, creating public-works programs—the building of the Central Highway and the elaborate Capitol building—and restricting sugar production in a failed attempt to benefit the island by controlling the world price. But in 1928, he amended the Constitution, elected himself to a six-year term, and turned himself into a Latin American *caudillo*—a strongman who would leave behind a memorable legacy of corruption and carnage. More than three decades later, desiring another political redeemer, the Cubans would cheer for Fidel Castro as he entered Havana to the beat of his own patriotic march.

When Natica Clews and Manolo Revuelta first encountered General Machado, they had just returned from their honeymoon. The couple's sophistication, their cultivation, overwhelmed the dictator. Machado even offered to send them to

Doña Natica as a fanciful young matron

Paris, as his good-will ambassadors, when Manolo finished his law degree. But the fairy-tale moment, when Manolo and Natica would represent the splendor of their country, was never to be. The evening before his last examination in the law, Manolo Revuelta caroused with his friends. He passed out over his guitar, and spent the night outside Doña Natica's locked door. When he awakened on the following day, the examination was over, and so was his brilliant career.

The marriage was troubled from the start, although Doña Natica tried to believe that she was a contented wife. Sometimes it was easy, particularly when she wore a party dress and danced on the roof of the Hotel Seville, or when she went to the races at Oriental Park, which made her feel that a gambler could win—if not on a horse, then maybe on a beautiful man with a guitar. The conventional Doña Natica couldn't imagine that Manolo Revuelta wouldn't want the same things she wanted or that she couldn't change him. When Manolo couldn't bear the weight of his wife's expectations or the hard, demanding world outside, he took to partying, to philandering, and to drink.

Doña Natica found herself pregnant with her daughter, Naty, and this, for a time, seemed to compensate for the bad bargain she'd made in marriage. Eventually, though, Doña Natica became impatient, intolerant of her husband's every gesture. Sometimes Manolo would stand in the street outside their house and bow to his bride at her balcony, just before he serenaded her with his guitar. Naty Revuelta remembers from her childhood hearing that her father made elaborate, sweeping bows, as though he were D'Artagnan wearing a plumed hat. Sometimes he brought his friend Eusebio Delfín, the musician who was altering the very nature of the romantic *bolero*. Together, the two friends sang Eusebio's most enchanting song: "And You, What Have You Done?" The strains of that *bolero* might still have been echoing in 1929, when Doña Natica threw her husband out of the house for the last time.

I N T H E stone house, when lunch is announced, Doña Natica gestures to me with a regal wave of her blue-veined hand. She regrets that it's so late in being served. *"Las cosas de palacio van despacio."* ("State matters, 'palace affairs,' move so slowly.") It doesn't matter. She sits down as if to a meal at the Miramar Restaurant in 1928: succulent native oysters, a delicious crawfish, an omelet browned in butter with delicate, powdered sugar, as celestial accompaniment a full-bodied Marqués de Riscal. She doesn't notice that she's actually only having a traditional *arroz con pollo.*

A challenged, resolute woman, Doña Natica has a strength that comes from a mixture of self-righteousness, pride, and an almost religious fervor about what might have been. On this visit, as on others, I felt somewhat manipulated, pressed to accept Doña Natica's own version of history. In telling the tale, she retained, or owned, her world. Wanting support from Naty, she was enraged at her daughter's resistance—her fluid movement into a story so different from her own. Soon I understood that, if what I wrote failed to please her, she would feel that I had betrayed her, too.

Doña Natica's own romantic fling had ended in ruin, forcing her to conclude that great passion imperiled a woman, hindered her search for long-term happiness. After the failure of her marriage, she had retreated to the nursery—a child under the bedcovers wanting safety, fearing the jungle on the other side of the sheets. Outside, the battle for *frijoles,* the strains of Eusebio Delfín's *bolero*; inside, the children dressed in white, a tamarind tree in the garden, the promenade along the Prado.

Naty's mother hoards her rescue fantasies, serving them to

me as soon as I'm seated at the table. Had Naty remained married, Orlando would have smuggled the family from the island, toasted their reunion with vintage glasses of champagne. Shaking a trembling fist, Doña Natica turns on her scapegoat, drenches her with recrimination: "My daughter doesn't understand because she's a Communist."

Her daughter invites anger. She hasn't set the table with Herbert Clews' silver, or the delicate, strawberry-banded Wedgwood, or the goblets presented years ago to Naty by the fabulous Frankie Steinhardt, an American industrialist who partied in Havana. Naty punctuates the air with her own acute frustration: "Mother wants the house to run as though we still had five servants." With her long history of indenture—first to her husband, then to Fidel—Naty resents being her mother's overworked parlormaid.

The Afro-Cuban "maid," Isora—a woman audacious enough to call Doña Natica "comrade"—provides the perspective. She has roasted a scrawny, hard-to-find black-market chicken, made some *moros y cristianos* ("Moors and Christians," a mixture of black beans and white rice), and served a yellow bread roll made of sweet-potato skins. She'd wanted to prepare a saffron rice, dousing the white grains with a popular kidney medicine that leaves everything an acrid orange, but she didn't dare. Who knew what the medication would do to Doña Natica, who was so fragile?

Doña Natica insists that Isora wouldn't know how to prepare a gourmet meal even with the right ingredients. How could she? There's so little food available to those who, like her, haven't a source of American dollars. Last Saturday, Isora's friends had wondered what they'd had for dinner. They knew it wasn't the promised rabbit. Her own ration card entitles Isora not to a chicken but to a baby chick; she walks it around the block at night on a home-made leash. When it's grown, Isora will have her own feast.

Isora worries that, if the Cuban-American exiles return, she and her family will be back at the bottom of the pile. Where will her family live when the *gusanos* come back across the straits, the deeds to their houses clutched in their hands? Will Doña Natica and her friends again wrap themselves in their winter furs and reconvene at El Carmelo for afternoons of hot chocolate and *churros?*

Doña Natica doesn't seem to notice when Isora clears the table. And, out of the blue, she begins to talk of Naty, as though her antagonist weren't there. She recounts how she had edged her daughter into the best Havana society—a confection of spun sugar. At the Condesa de Revilla de Camargo's dinner for the Princesse de Rethy, Naty and three hundred other guests had dined on plates of solid gold. (One of Naty's friends wrote of the evening: "It was a dream from which none of us wanted to awaken.") Before she went into exile, the Condesa hid the gold inside a false wall in her house. The servants soon found the precious stash and turned it over to the government.

When Fidel marched into Havana, Doña Natica didn't believe that the boat was rocking. She was like one of those carefree passengers on the *Titanic* who danced on the first-class deck even after the liner collided with the fatal iceberg. But, Doña Natica recounts, her favorite brother, Bebo, had warned the family that Fidel was a Communist when he was still in the Sierra Maestra. Fidel may have worn rosary beads around his throat as he entered Havana, but his thoughts were wholly secular. Doña Natica remembers that Bebo, a Cuban diplomat, had perspicaciously christened the guerrilla movement *"la revolución de melón"*—green on the outside, red on the inside.

Her mother's words condemn Naty to the tedious business

of defending her past. "We were all in love with Fidel. What happened to me happened to the whole country. Infatuated, we followed him along forbidden paths, trusting him, feeling our way." Just under her breath, Doña Natica is muttering: *"Más vale estar solo que mal acompañado."* ("Better to be alone than in bad company.") Since a woman can't take care of herself, she must be delivered into the arms of a suitable man who will protect her. That's the implication. Doña Natica won't openly admit that women need to be rescued. But she warms to my story of Edith Wharton's heroine Lily Bart, who takes an overdose of chloral because she neither can find a husband to take care of her nor has the inner resources to live on her own.

Then Doña Natica delivers a story of her own. It is about Nena Mañach, the Havana socialite, who would never have consigned herself, to say nothing of her family, to the rented room where Wharton's Lily Bart commits suicide. Nena's story, an allegory of success, stands in implicit counterpoint to the sad tale of Naty Revuelta.

At the age of eighteen, the lively and dark-eyed Nena Mañach gave little thought to her beauty and charm. She liked to climb into her brother's Hispano-Suiza and drive into the countryside, where she could ride horses. On the bridle path one morning, she met the Marqués de Aguas Claras—a dashing young aristocrat who smoked Dimitrino cigarettes and affected coats of Chinese silk. They soon became engaged. The engagement lasted, however, only until Nena's mother discovered that her future son-in-law was partly black—a Marqués of Aguas Sucias (Dirty, Muddy Waters), said her horrified friends.

At a farewell meeting, a tearful Nena announced, "We can't marry each other because we belong to different races." Overcome with grief, the young man put a pistol to his head; fortunately, Nena's brothers arrived in time to disarm him.

(After the revolution, the Marqués de Aguas Claras used to wander around the Plaza de Armas, his sorrowful face covered with a dreadful white powder.)

On an impulse, Nena married an irresponsible Italian aristocrat, whom she divorced soon after their daughter's birth. To save this young woman who couldn't fend for herself, Nena's friends set about finding the right husband for her. ("They didn't start agitating for a Communist revolution," Doña Natica points out, "just because things were difficult.") On the evening of Andrew Goodman's arrival at the Havana Yacht Club, Nena, her head held high, made a stunning entrance in a borrowed Lanvin dress and her grandmother's oyster pearls. Marriage followed in New York, where Andrew worked for Bergdorf Goodman, the family-owned department store; Nena returned to Havana only for the parties of the winter season. After the revolution, she arranged for a parade of exiled socialites to work at Bergdorf's. To friends who remained in Havana, Nena sent packages of dresses, silk stockings, and her favorite designer shoes.

Doña Natica reveres Nena Mañach. She wishes that her own daughter had had a smattering of Nena's common sense; but instead Naty harbored fantasies that unraveled in a cautionary tale of passion. Doña Natica is not at all surprised that Nena Mañach Goodman, surrounded by her family, lives in great state on Fifth Avenue in New York while Naty Revuelta, without her daughters or grandchildren, struggles along in Havana, standing in line for hours to obtain a rationed pound of *frijoles negros*.

DOÑA NATICA delivers her lines with authority. "When you come to visit me again," she tells me as I'm leaving, "if I'm not at home, you'll find me in the Chinese cemetery. It's just across the street. When I die, there won't be enough gas to get me to the family plot at the Colón. I'll just have to count on the Chinese. At least, I can be sure that Fidel won't be there." A smile. *"De todos modos, me gustan los chinos."* ("In any case, I'm fond of the Chinese.") Doña Natica repeats her words, enjoying their effect. *"¡Qué pena!* [What a shame!] I always thought I'd be buried in a huge mausoleum. . . ."

After living in Havana throughout more than three decades of Fidel Castro's regime, Doña Natica has come to believe that she might feel more at home in China. She feels, after all, an affinity for ancient Chinese ladies—their arches broken, their feet tightly bound—who hobble around the miniature enclosures that have become their entire worlds.

For the most part, Naty Revuelta doesn't hear her mother's words, and perhaps it's a good thing, because their domestic truce is so fragile. A single careless word can shatter the household for the rest of the day, sending Doña Natica to her room in tears, pushing Naty, and her ever-present lighted cigarette, out the front door and into the heat of the street. *"Me quiere enterrar."* ("She wants to bury me.")

Most of the people who shared Doña Natica's vanished world have gone. And Doña Natica has never accepted that, not really. When Fidel Castro marched into Havana, many of her friends put down their canasta cards, locked the gates to their houses, and followed their children into exile.

After more than three decades—and the dissolution of the rest of the Communist world—Fidel Castro still clings to the island, and Doña Natica can't seem to make much sense of what has happened. Her friends have never returned; in most cases, their sadness has already accompanied them to their deaths. Of necessity, Doña Natica has retreated into her remembered world, where she has found a means of survival. Outside this magic circle, there's nothing but a harsh and unfamiliar place. Doña Natica is in exile there—isolated, fractured, unanchored—even though she's never left Havana.

At the Cementerio de Cristóbal Colón, the necropolis near the Almendares River, Doña Natica's world has enshrined itself. Colonial aristocrats, students massacred by the Spanish, politicians who raided the national treasury, rebellious artists, worthy burghers, poseurs, courtesans—all rest together in this strange nineteenth-century city of the dead. There is even a tomb for Cecilia Valdés, heroine of the island's most celebrated romantic novel. You can read much of the island's history in the pantheons of Carrara marble, in the positioning of the tombs to reflect the social standing of the deceased.

Funerals at the Colón were once extravagant, pretentious rites of passage. Men dressed in scarlet swallow-tailed coats, with silver buckles on their shoes, guided elaborate horse-drawn hearses through the triumphal arch that dominates the cemetery's entrance. Now the ruined monuments of the merchants and the nobles are a final reminder of the pomp and circumstance that surrounded their dead: the Falla Bonets lie in their stone replicas of the Egyptian pyramids. Miguel González de Mendoza, a sentimentalist among financiers, slumbers in imitation of Michelangelo's *Pietà*. The Conde de Rivero, a man whose enthusiasms ran to the pursuit of young women, rests attended by a choir of marble damsels. Juana Martine, who devoted her life to the game of dominoes, lies beneath the granite replica of an ivory double-three. Her son and daughter had found that tile clutched in her hand at the moment of her death. In the 1920s, the Colón cemetery was informally called *el último paradero*, the "last stop," because the bus route ended there. In the nineties, it's a museum of memories set in stone.

But nothing remains truly static. Even at the Colón cemetery, one woman has finally entered into the flow of the present. Now called *la milagrosa*, she died a conventional *bourgeoise* and was buried beneath an atrocious alabaster statue of a mother and child. Legend has it that when she was removed from the ground—nobody seems to care why she was disturbed—she emerged from her grave flawless, intact. Soon, people began to turn to "the miraculous one" for favors.

A sense of the present: An Afro-Cuban *santera*, kneeling in this Catholic cemetery, instigates a sacred collusion with the long-dead white woman. Realities change; narratives interpenetrate. At the tomb of *la milagrosa,* roses, gladiolas, and gardenias, rare in Havana, surround the marble statue of a mother and child. *"Milagrosa, por favor . . . necesito una casa, un trabajo. . . ."* ("Miracle worker, please . . . I need a house, a job. . . .")

But the legend of *la milagrosa* doesn't illuminate the story of Doña Natica. In fact, Doña Natica is not attracted to that legend, because it is too densely Caribbean. She prefers the story of Catalina Lasa, her beautiful, pampered, fortunate friend. For Doña Natica, there is nothing more miraculous than the rounded crystal covering that the French sculptor René Lalique designed for Catalina's sepulcher, especially when the sun catches the dome, and the image of the famous Catalina Lasa rose becomes visible on the crystal surface. Catalina Lasa's second husband, Juan Pedro Baró, insisted on being buried alongside his wife in a standing position, so that he could continue to protect her.

Society was not amused when Catalina Lasa, the most exciting woman in Havana, abandoned her first husband, Luis Estevez, and ran away to Paris with her wealthy lover, Juan Pedro Baró. Havana, in the twenties, was not particularly forgiving of marital scandals among the female members of its bourgeoisie; retribution and contrition were demanded in return for forgiveness. Marianita Seva, the Cuban president's wife, was overheard to say: *"Lo único bueno que tiene Catalina es su terno de esmeraldas."* ("The only good thing about Catalina is her emerald tiara.")

Catalina's angry mother-in-law, Marta Abréu, a member of the eccentric clan who lived at Las Delicias—a house modeled on an English castle, where chimpanzees were trained as servants—arrived at Catalina's residence, threw her clothes out the bedroom window, and auctioned her lingerie on the street below. Still filled with righteous indignation, Marta arranged for the French police to enter the lovers' hotel suite and accuse Juan Pedro of adultery. "But there is no one here," lied the honorable gentleman, "except the wife of Juan Pedro Baró." As soon as he could, Juan Pedro married Catalina. They lived in Paris for the next few years, and when Catalina wanted to return to her country, her besotted husband built her the most beautiful house in Havana.

The stunning Art Deco mansion—these very modern lovers turned their backs on the Baroque tastes favored by the rich in Havana—featured a formal staircase of red Languedoc marble, chandeliers by René Lalique, and grilled iron railings designed in Paris by the house of Baguez. It was a truth universally agreed upon that the sand used in the construction of the house had come from the River Nile.

When the house was finished, Juan Pedro and Catalina decided to open the season with a huge dance and to invite *le tout Havana*. Although society had been prepared to decline the invitation of the scandalous couple, when the engraved cards were received, each containing a valuable bauble, everyone's mind was changed. The party was a great success; Havana found it even more pleasurable to dance than to censure. Catalina Lasa and Juan Pedro commanded a place at the very center of Havana society until Catalina's unfortunate death after eating a poisoned oyster at the Ritz in Paris.

In Catalina's life, Doña Natica stumbles on a redeemed

version of her own. Perhaps it's because their education was similar—their training in needlepoint, their resignation to traditional, inherited roles. The story of Doña Natica's childhood, coming of age, and marriage underlines the dangers of a life with limited strategies for survival. Doña Natica envies her friend, loves the story of Catalina Lasa, because it is another narrative of recovery.

Because she was rescued, Catalina rests in a marble tomb, while a fragile, unloved Doña Natica trudges along on the road to the Chinese cemetery.

Doña Natica and her husband, Manolo Revuelta

Naty and her father, Manolo, just before the divorce

CHAPTER 4

The Transformation of Naty

NOTHING would ever be as exciting, not even her future romance with Fidel Castro, as the moment when Natalia Revuelta Clews first saw her father again. On the evening of February 28, 1930, at the Teatro Payret in Havana, Ernesto Lecuona inaugurated his musical season with a program of *zarzuelas*—the light romantic operettas that Cubans loved. Doña Natica, who took four-year-old Naty to the concert, wore a blue silk dress and her sapphire-and-diamond brooch; the little girl wore white organdy and, in her loose auburn hair, a green ribbon that almost exactly matched her eyes.

During the intermission, Manolo Revuelta emerged from the back of the theatre, bowed to his estranged wife, and embraced the small daughter he hadn't seen for a year. When he held her in his arms, Manolo told Naty that she was beautiful and that he loved her very much. But as soon as the evening was over, this father whom the little girl had begun again to adore simply vanished into the night.

Each year, when Ernesto Lecuona gave his concert of *zarzuelas,* Naty went to the Teatro Payret with her mother; and each time, her father was there to see her. These meetings resembled a sort of sacred ceremony in three acts—the appearance, the embrace, the departure—and it had a lasting effect on the little girl. Natalia Revuelta Clews would always long for the romantic, insecure world of her father. That passionate connection to a man who both enchanted and abandoned her, that blurred image of love, would determine the curve of her emotional future.

AT THE moment of Naty Revuelta's birth, on December 6, 1925, in a private clinic in Havana, there were no cribs available. Someone thought to place the infant in a narrow bureau drawer in her mother's hospital room. Much later, Naty imagined that her friends had been delivered into graceful, golden cradles, where they could breathe free, whereas she had arrived to be immured, almost suffocated, in an airless wooden chest. The story has served Naty well; it dramatizes, adds poignancy to, her sense of herself as being prematurely buried in her mother's house, condemned to search for love outside its walls.

When Naty's world first crumbled, she was only three years old. But she would remember the day for the rest of her life, as though she were still fragile in the face of it. "One afternoon, my father asked my mother to meet him at a hotel near the Prado. I guess he was living there temporarily. I'm not sure. But I remember sitting on a bed with them. I was in the middle and both of them were crying. My father put his arms around me. I was sitting there, numbed, watching the scene, as though it had nothing to do with me. Even now, I remember the feeling of numbness."

Doña Natica, at the insistence of her father, had decided to end the marriage long before the encounter in the hotel. One morning, while walking past his daughter's house, Herbert Clews had seen Manolo passed out and straddling the front door. He crossed over the sleeping body and told his daughter that she could no longer live with an irresponsible alcoholic. That evening, Doña Natica separated from her husband and returned to her father's house.

With little difficulty, the young woman fell back into the comforting, measured rhythms in which she had been raised, in a house where the accents were English and the sounds of guitars muted—and where, once again, household routines bolstered the illusion of safety. Each morning, Doña Natica had her *café con leche* with her father while her mother sat beside them in silent accompaniment. When they had finished, Herbert put fifteen pesos on the table for the *cocinera* to take to the vegetable market. This simple ritual calmed his daughter's fears. Doña Natica often thought of the heavy-breasted *cocinera* and of onions, carrots, and parsley.

Manolo Revuelta, save for those fleeting concert reunions and the occasional meeting by chance, vanished forever from the life of his daughter. Forsaking Havana, he established himself in the province of Oriente, on the eastern end of the island, as an inspector of sugar mills. Naty never mentioned him to her mother, but she nurtured a clandestine passion for the handsome fugitive. Decades later, he would return to Havana, marry again, and settle for an uncomplicated, boring existence. Whenever she encountered him, Naty deluded herself that her father was a god disguised as an ordinary man.

In the defining moment, when her father disappeared, Naty Revuelta experienced the connection between passion and abandonment. Perhaps that would explain how, after her own marriage, she could dismiss a faithful husband and focus instead on a careless, absent lover. In her mind, there was an opposition between the cold, rational plane inhabited by her mother and the warm, passionate corner of her heart where she visited with her father. To compensate for the pain involved in loving someone who was absent, Naty would create a rich, textured, inner landscape where she lived with Manolo Revuelta. In the same world, one filled with music and sunlight, she would dance with Fidel after he, too, had left her forever.

NATY'S American Havana was coming of age while the little girl was learning to walk. Spanish Havana, with its patios, wooden balconies, and barred windows—a place that resembled nothing so much as a provincial town in Castile—had lingered well into the second decade of the twentieth century. Until then, most of the streets were unpaved: cows and goats sauntered along the narrow paths in the ancient quarter; the street vendors' sounds were deafening, duels for the sake of honor were not uncommon, and most of the women remained hidden behind iron grilles.

As late as 1927, Joseph Hergesheimer, an American traveler, found Havana's charm in her evocation of the past: "Spain," he wrote, "touched by the tropics." An idler himself, Hergesheimer liked nothing more than to inhale a Dimitrino cigarette and promenade along the crowded streets. He wrote of his pleasure in the *glorietas,* the outdoor cafés, the gatherings along the Paseo del Prado and along the curving seaside Malecón. The bewitched Northerner delighted in "the shifting radiance" of colored fanlights on the houses, the parterres of flowers and palms, the statues, the fountains, the alfresco concerts where the band played the light arias of *La Belle Hélène.* In the late afternoon, he watched the sun set on frosted buildings that turned lavender, and then a glimmering white.

Independence from Spain, together with the cultural influence of the United States, was bringing the curtain down on

Hergesheimer's graceful Havana. Doña Natica might remember the city of her birth with nostalgia, but it was vanishing like the *volanta* and the *calesero*. Huge American investment had resulted in an economic boom which stimulated the city's transformation—a process that began during World War I with "the dance of the millions." Cuba, the leading producer of sugar, whirled and whirled as the global price of sugar soared. It was the time of the fatted calves, and the city changed forever.

Social, caricaturist Conrado Massaguer's modernist periodical popular in the twenties and thirties, attracted sophisticated Cubans who were bored with their colonial heritage and drawn to the lifestyle of the American bourgeoisie. María Luisa Lobo, a Cuban writer, has described Massaguer's creation of the thoroughly modern Cuban Massa-Girl—a Creole flapper based on the American girls emancipated at the end of World War I. "The girl he drew was young and pretty, very much into the style of her times: she loved sports, led an independent life, smoked and drank in public places, dressed in the latest fashions."

In the pages of *Social*, American companies and products beckon to susceptible Cuban consumers: La Nueva Radio-Electrola Victor; Ford Motor Company; Hotpoint; Del Monte; Kellogg's Corn Flakes; El Nuevo Cine Kodak. Jabón Facial Woodbury promised that you can live on a tropical island and still have a complexion that enchants. The National City Bank of New York asked: *¿Qué sucederá si no deja Ud. un testamento?*" ("What will happen if you don't leave a will?")

Havana Mañana, a fashionable American travel guide published later, in 1941, revealed a city that would have sent the fastidious Joseph Hergesheimer reeling. "Today, daughters of Cuba's first families lounge or play on the clubhouse grounds with the same freedom our own girls enjoy. . . ." The authors advised women who were traveling to the island that Havana was about fun, flirtation, and seduction. In Havana, "no matter where you go or how you look, you are followed by a chorus of *"Ay, ¡qué linda!* ("How beautiful!") *"¡Sabrosísima!"* ("Delicious!") and *"¡Qué carita más preciosa!"* ("What an exquisite face!")

From across the Straits of Florida, the Americans brought not only their money but their fantasies of the good life: *el country club, el golf course.* The *tertulias*—the small nineteenth-century gatherings around which the patricians had structured their social lives, sometimes with theatricals—and the Saturday evenings "at home" were replaced by far more more elaborate festivities: *los cocktails, los dinners, los bridge parties.* The Cubans, eager to change partners, abandoned their Spanish *contradanzas* for *el American two-step* and *el foxtrot.* The Havana woman turned in her lace mantilla for a fashionable turban and marched out the door in a pair of sling-back high heels.

NATY REVUELTA remembers a day when she was still small and her mother took her downtown to do some shopping. They wandered past stores ranging from El Encanto to Woolworth's. Naty, walking ahead of her mother, peered into the windows of the festive shops. Woolworth's sold baby chicks in little white cardboard boxes; Naty was fascinated by how small they were, so easy to crush.

When she had finished pressing her nose against the glass pane, the little girl looked around and found that Doña Natica wasn't there. She grew terrified, raced up and down the street, calling over and over again for her mother. She was frightened, crazed, darting about in vain. Just when her world seemed to have fallen apart, her mother emerged from her hiding place, laughing, looking as though she enjoyed the fear she had caused in her small daughter. With a mocking flourish, she cried, "I'm here! I'm here!"

(When I heard this story, it touched me. As a child, visiting Havana with my grandmother, I had awakened in the middle of the night and called to her. I remember the oppressive heat and the mosquito netting that shrouded her sleeping figure. She wouldn't answer. I crept out of my bed, a snare of white gauzy mosquito netting, and climbed into hers. I pushed and pulled at her arms; I covered her face with kisses; I demanded that she speak to me. How was I to know if she was alive? But there was no answer. Finally, when I collapsed in uncontrollable sobs, I heard her voice: *"¿Qué harías sin mí?"* ["Without me, what would become of you?"])

After the incident downtown, Naty was never comfortable with Doña Natica. She rejects the idea of any surviving tenderness between them. That early memory of her mother would stand in counterpoint to the story of her father at the Ernesto Lecuona concert, underlining the differences between her parents. But perhaps her mother hadn't intended the gratuitous cruelty. She may simply have indulged herself in the need to feel, for a moment, that she had some power, whereas most of the time she felt impotent. Raising her daughter, riding the high waves alone, Doña Natica more often than not felt tossed in the air and returned to the shore, bruised and beaten.

Only a few months after the Woolworth's debacle, the almost unthinkable happened: Herbert Clews died (of uremic poisoning, at Georgetown Hospital in Washington, D.C.). To make matters worse, when the lawyers looked into Herbert's estate, they found nothing but debts and obligations. In a Dickensian twist, the family's trusted accountant had absconded with his charges' funds. The widow would have to make do

Naty and her mother

Herbert Clews, his daughter, Doña Natica, and a friend,
in Virginia shortly before his death

with a small pension. Doña Natica was forced to confront the world without her main protector.

Doña Natica could have run to her brothers for cover, but she didn't. Instead, in a fierce decision to redeem her shattered existence through her daughter's, she dedicated herself to making sure that Naty became invulnerable—a woman who wouldn't ever feel the ground give way beneath her feet. A photograph of Doña Natica in a white dress, holding her father's hand—not the tinted image of herself as Manolo's bride—evoked the heaven she was burnishing for her daughter.

WHEN Naty was a child, there was an orphanage in Havana called La Beneficencia, founded by Bishop Valdés in the eighteenth century. All the children who were brought there received the surname of Valdés, in tribute to the cleric's kindness and generosity. At the side door, there was a revolving contraption. The mother would ring a bell, and the turnstile deposited the baby inside the building. In that instant of transformation, La Beneficencia preserved the mother's anonymity, assumed responsibility for the child, and established another identity for the infant.

Naty's mother had something similar in mind, another sort of transformation, when she deposited her thirteen-year-old daughter at Mount St. Joseph's Academy in Chestnut Hill, outside of Philadelphia. After her divorce and, later, her father's death, Doña Natica reassessed her situation. She felt that Havana was turning into an American colony, and, a practical woman, she determined to educate her daughter to take her place in it.

Blessed with great beauty and a flirtatious nature, Doña Natica managed to take advantage of these attributes to secure a reliable, non-guitar-playing second husband. In 1935, when she married Herberto Coll, an executive for the U.S.-owned Havana Electric Company, she offered him her faithfulness and devotion in return for his financial protection. Doña Natica no longer believed in love. She needed a man, not for herself, but for her daughter's benefit. Without Herberto, Doña Natica couldn't have sent Naty to school in the United States. *"Tengo que preparar a Naty."* ("Naty must be prepared.") With that noble mission in mind, Doña Natica was free to impose her will on a husband and a daughter in both of whom she aroused a fierce resentment.

Doña Natica's dreams for her daughter never failed to elude her. Rosita Coll, Herberto's own live-in daughter, might have been a better candidate for transformation: an elegant blonde with long slim legs inherited from her bolting American mother. Naty, on the other hand, was thoroughly Cuban, and likely to remain so. She had a sultriness about her, more than a suggestion of passion in her green eyes. The two young women might have been figures in a fairy tale: Rosita's pale, fair beauty contrasted with Naty's tawnier earthiness. After the revolution, Rosita Coll would cross the straits and settle in Florida with her husband. Naty, in love with Fidel, chose to remain in Havana.

AT MOUNT St. Joseph's Academy, religion became a release for Naty's ardent spirit. With the same fervor she would later direct towards Fidel, the young girl turned her face towards God. "I wanted to be a nun," she told me. "Sister Claire Helene. I really had a crush on her. All the time I was there, I wanted to be a nun. But then it ended." With her need for a purpose larger than herself, she read Somerset Maugham's *The Razor's Edge* three times. The novel spoke to her own desire to transcend bourgeois expectations and commit herself to a cause worthy of her passionate nature.

A few small narrative changes to the story of her forebears and Naty could see herself as the inheritor of a proud tradition of Cuban patriotism. She forgot that her father played *boleros* on his guitar and began remembering him as a vocal supporter of the trade-union movement. She thought about Herbert Clews, who had fought against Spain with the rebel *mambises* in '95, and of her grandmother Natalia, who had attached ribbons of red, white, and blue to her dresses in honor of the Cuban flag. But how to add another chapter?

When her year of schooling in Philadelphia ended, Naty returned to Havana, where she read her grandfather's copy of José Martí's biography. A Cuban Don Quixote, a romantic intellectual, Martí was shot to death in 1895 as he charged into battle astride his white horse. His insistence that Cuba maintain an identity separate from that of the United States made him a heroic figure long after the end of the war for independence.

Naty loved Martí's words, the strong feelings he expressed against the country in which she had spent two school semesters. "I know the Monster because I have lived in its lair—and my weapon is only the slingshot of David." What was one to make of this? Some people said that Cuba had the shape of a *caimán*, an alligator with a long tail, playfully flicking at Florida. But it didn't seem that way to Naty Revuelta. The United States was more like Martí's Monster, carrying the entire distraught Cuban alligator between its teeth.

In the late thirties, when Naty was at school in Philadelphia, the Silver Meteor traveled daily between New York and Miami, at the special rate of $40.35 for a fifteen-day round trip. A complete dinner could be had for only sixty cents. The chairs reclined at night, and for twenty-five cents you could reserve a pillow. Passengers were advised that a hostess was on duty at all times, in case anyone felt the need for companionship. The

Meteor connected to an overnight Peninsular and Occidental Steamship Company boat, which went back and forth between Havana and Miami four times a week. For only four dollars more, tourists could soar above the straits on a Silver Clipper flight and watch the light dancing on the clear blue water beneath.

The boundaries that separated the island from the mainland were so blurred that it was hard, on arriving in Havana, to tell that one was no longer in Florida. Americans didn't even need a passport to travel to the island. If you were more comfortable taking your car, you could put it on the boat and drive it around the island, knowing that an American driver's license and registration papers were all that was necessary. At the Anglo-American Hospital, everyone spoke English. Prescriptions could be filled at Dr. Lorie's American Drug Store. You could spend the evening watching American movies, or reading the news in the *Havana Post*—published, of course, in English.

Naty would spend the three years following her return from Philadelphia at Ruston Academy in Havana—an American school (Miles Standish was the name of one of the yearbook's editors) founded to prepare its best students for Harvard, Yale, and Princeton. The school educated primarily the growing numbers of both American and Cuban children whose parents worked for U.S. companies. (General Batista's son would attend Ruston in the 1950s.) In 1993, at a gala reunion at the Sevilla-Biltmore Hotel in Coral Gables, the graduates of Ruston Academy fantasized putting the school together again. Most of the alumni agreed that Fidel Castro's revolution was an unfortunate interlude in the history of the school.

When Naty acted in the school production of Honorio Maura's *Cuento de Hadas,* the consensus was that her lamentations were worthy of Eleanora Duse and Sarah Bernhardt. In the "last will and testament of the senior class," it was noted that "Natty Revuelta leaves her magnetism to whoever needs it." For the class photograph, her expression is serious and she wears her mother's string of pearls. Underneath the picture, the caption reads: "She has more than beauty, she has *It*."

Naty graduated from Ruston Academy with the class of 1943. For the two years that followed, she studied at Marjorie Webster Junior College in Washington, D.C., where she perfected her American English. She returned to Havana in 1945, educated and marriageable.

Once more in Doña Natica's orbit, Naty found herself a job at the U.S. Embassy's Immigration Section and proceeded to wait, as young women did, for the man of her dreams. It was not hard to go to the embassy every day, accompany important visitors to the Hotel Nacional for lunch, and type the letters assigned to her each morning. But it was pointless, boring. Naty spent hours cleaning the desk drawers, putting rubber bands around the pencils, making sure the erasure rubbings weren't visible. When no one was looking, she would devote herself to reading José Martí. "A nation," he wrote, "is not a complex of wheels, nor a wild horse race, but a stride upward concerted by real men."

Naty wasn't certain what she wanted, but she had a bent for romantic causes and a susceptibility to the music that might suit those struggles. On her return from Washington, she told her mother that she planned to devote her leisure hours to the harp. Doña Natica, trembling with shock, forbade her daughter to involve herself with that strange and cumbersome instrument. After all that education, how could her daughter want only to wear a long dress, a fragrant gardenia in her hair, while playing Debussy's "Le Cygne" on the harp? She was just like her father.

Not that Doña Natica was against music. But what about the piano, a musical instrument that so many people had in their houses, or even the guitar, which Naty could carry with her to an evening party? A harp would cost almost as much as an Oldsmobile. And each time she was invited to play it, she'd have to hire a truck and sit next to the chauffeur. Doña Natica never considered the music itself; her daughter buried her feelings and never mentioned the harp to her mother again.

In 1947, Doña Natica was a startlingly beautiful woman just beginning to surrender her youth. Sitting in a trolley car staring out the window one spring day that year, she remembered the time Manolo Revuelta, a man who loved his wine, had recited poetry to her as he swayed dangerously in the narrow space between two trolley cars. He might have fallen under the wheels, maimed himself, died in the accident. Doña Natica couldn't forget that she had found his performance embarrassing. She was much more pleased with her second husband, Herberto Coll, who had probably never voluntarily read a poem but at least paid her daughter's tuition.

On this May afternoon, Doña Natica was on her way to a fitting at the Casa de Bernabeo, and her thoughts turned to clothes. She was thrilled with Ismael Bernabeo, a designer whose hands molded silks and satins into dresses of incomparable beauty; Havana compared him to Paris's Balenciaga. When Doña Natica wore one of the master's evening dresses, she resembled her best imagining of herself—the grand and stylish daughter of Herbert Clews, dancing to an American band on the rooftop of the Hotel Almendares.

Suddenly, in the middle of her reverie, Doña Natica was startled by a glimpse of her daughter, who was descending a nearby trolley. Naty looked pale, frightened, her lips green and swollen, and clearly very ill. Doña Natica got off her trolley at the next stop and tried to catch up with Naty on the way back to their house. When she arrived, she found her daughter feverish and on the verge of collapse.

Doña Natica called her husband, Herberto, who came in his car and rushed them all to the Centro Médico in the Vedado. The diagnosis was peritonitis and a perforated appendix. Dr. José Bisbee, the attending surgeon, emerged frowning from the operating theatre. He told the frightened Doña Natica that he was quite certain her daughter would die. "When the doctors opened me up," Naty told me, "everything just burst. The surgeon powdered the womb with sulfa, closed me up again, and hoped for the best." As she described the incident, her tone was matter-of-fact. "I'm not dramatic," she said, " but my life is a great drama."

Naty's marriage both directly and indirectly proceeded from her experience in cheating death. Before that crisis, Naty was spontaneous, even careless. Her bout with mortality made her believe that living was as dangerous as her mother had always told her it might be.

Dr. Bisbee, with a daughter Naty's age, had not been able to face the imminent death of this beautiful young woman alone. He arranged a medical consultation with his friend Dr. Orlando Fernández, an eminent cardiologist. Looking at Naty lying unconscious in her hospital bed, Dr. Fernández refused to let her die and felt that he would never again want to leave her side. When Naty Revuelta opened her eyes, she was staring at her future husband. A man almost twenty years older than she, Orlando had a round face, a small mustache, thinning black hair, and gentle brown eyes that seemed to dissolve when he smiled. Even Doña Natica, who delighted in her prospective son-in-law, was forced to admit that he resembled Agatha Christie's Hercule Poirot, the detective with the egg-shaped head, and not, as a woman of that era might have wished, Ronald Colman or Douglas Fairbanks.

Still, Orlando had rescued Naty, and that, of course, set him apart from her other suitors. *"Aquellos ojos verdes serenos, "* he sang to her, *"dejaron en mi alma / eterna sed de amar."* ("Those serene green eyes have given my soul an eternal thirst to love.") That he was a doctor seemed so distinguished, and ennobling. For a moment, Naty was able to give Orlando a place in her heart very near the corner she'd reserved for José Martí.

Reducing the world to black and white, Naty created a reality in which moral choice was obvious. Orlando in his white coat, making his medical rounds, won an easy victory over her other suitors—the dilettantes whose white linen suits were suitable for nothing more distinctive than strutting and preening. In her mind, Naty elevated and sanctified Orlando; marriage to such a distinguished healer would create a union of two noble spirits. At the same time, she solved a practical problem. Social reality had confined her either to finding a husband—and the prospects for that had never been exciting—or to living with her dictatorial, argumentative mother.

When Orlando and Naty married a few months later, it was agreed that the fashionable Bernabeo, who made the bride's wedding dress, a fragile creation of ivory silk and Alençon lace, had more than outdone himself. At the Vedado Parish Church, the altar was covered with masses of white tea roses. Naty had wanted lilies of the valley, but Doña Natica insisted on tea roses, her own father's favorite.

Her mind occupied with thoughts of innocent pleasures, Naty seemed destined for an agreeable, conventional life. Still in her early twenties, she was beginning to tame her youthful beauty, to harness and deliver it into the hands of an eager society. At the Vedado Tennis Club, she played mixed doubles and then lunched with her partners on the terrace. For fashion events, she was considered the most glamorous of society models. More than one dress was sold to a man who believed that an expensive costume could turn his plump wife into the feline Naty Revuelta.

In the fifties, Havana was decadent—it's true—but it was fast, racy, and fun. She lured the young with *boleros*, with *mambós* and the *cha-cha-cha*, seduced the visitor with extravagant nightclub productions. At the Tropicana, the famous cabaret, long-limbed *mulatas* sauntered across the stage, wearing glittering chandeliers on their heads. During Carnival, Naty's friends would hire some of the boxes that the city had erected along the Prado to watch the *comparsas*—the bands of *negros* dancing in the street, their lanterns swirling in the night air. *En La Habana se permite todo menos ser pesado.* (In Havana, anything goes, as long as you're not a bore.)

Could anyone forget the balls? Annamaría Crossfield's father once dressed as the Emperor Nero, carrying a fiddle, and wearing a box of matches pinned to his toga. For Chea Pedroso's Baile de las Piedras Preciosas, the guests were asked to come dressed as their own birthstones. Annamaría, whose aunt had traveled to Paris and returned with the red glass beads to sew into her dress, impersonated a sultan's ruby. Margarita Herrera glittered as a diamond in white chiffon and sparkles. A dramatic Nelia Barletta entered the party as an onyx, elegant in black satin and feathers.

In the midst of the festivities, El Country Club held its annual Baile Rojo. Each year, the theme changed: the Gay Nineties, the Roaring Twenties, musical comedy, opera, the circus. One of its most successful events featured young socialites acting out scenes from various operas, lip-synching the arias that Renata Tebaldi and Joan Sutherland sang on phonograph records hidden behind the stage.

The young women were in rehearsal for months, while their mothers' seamstresses worked overtime to stitch the costumes that transformed them into Aida, Madame Butterfly, or, in Nelia Barletta's case, Violetta, in a white velvet dress trimmed with ermine. (When she left the country, after the revolution,

*Naty as "India"
at the Biltmore Country Club*

Naty modeling for charity

Nelia was allowed to take all of her clothes save the dress from the Baile Rojo. The immigration authorities couldn't believe it was part of a personal wardrobe.)

At a Biltmore Country Club Gala, with its most beautiful socialites representing different countries of the world, Naty was costumed as India: stunning, bejeweled, mysterious. General Batista, present at the spectacular, made discreet inquiries about the arresting India, but that was about as much danger as a woman like Naty ever faced. In the confines of the Biltmore—and her world was no larger than that—wearing a silk sari and a pair of golden slippers was as adventurous as Naty intended to get.

Soon after their marriage, Naty and Orlando had moved into a beautiful house in the Vedado. Though its formal elegance suggested that the couple might distinguish themselves as party-givers, nothing of the sort ever happened. Naty and Orlando seldom went out for an evening and almost never invited friends for dinner. On the rare occasion when they did entertain, Orlando, exhausted from his long hours at the clinic, almost immediately fell asleep in his chair.

Once, just before the guests were to arrive for dinner, Orlando called to tell Naty that he had to stay with a patient. She argued with him until he agreed to come home, but it wasn't a victory. Orlando was preoccupied, uninterested in the conversation—it was an ordeal for him even to sit at the table—and he excused himself several times to call the clinic.

Unimpressed by Naty's social friends, whom he found superficial, Orlando was not about to perform for them. This infuriated Naty, because her power and glory hadn't to do with her own achievement, but were conferred in a marriage to a distinguished man. What was the point of that marriage, after all—and, more important, who was she—if her eminent husband presented himself to others as nothing more than a tired, ordinary doctor?

There were those, particularly among Naty's friends, who agreed that Orlando was to blame for the tension in the marriage. Obsessed with medicine, the doctor gave little thought to the needs of a beautiful young wife. When he did have some time, he turned his attention to his demanding, domineering mother, whom he saw every day before he came home for dinner. For the most part, Naty spent the evenings at home alone, thumbing through her books or watching television. Orlando, when he thought about it at all, couldn't understand why she wasn't perfectly happy.

WHEN Naty became pregnant, she was thrilled and her husband was relieved. Raised among traditional women, Orlando took it for granted that his wife's fulfillment would come with the birth of a child. After that, all would be well. He would have what his mother had always told him an accomplished older man deserved: an undemanding wife who delighted in the children and created a calm, contented household for him.

But it wasn't that simple. Pregnant with her first child, Naty felt fragile, and unprotected. When Orlando went to Boston for almost three weeks—he accompanied his mother, who was to have surgery at the Leahy Clinic—and left his young wife alone, she felt utterly abandoned. She told me about it many years later, suggesting that her marriage never recovered from that separation. "I was frightened, insecure. Orlando had promised me he'd be gone for no more than seventy-two hours, but he didn't come back until his mother was ready to travel with him. He was gone for almost three weeks. It just wasn't acceptable."

While Orlando was in Boston with his mother, Naty

Revuelta slept with a large hatpin under her pillow. With the best of intentions, Orlando had hired a Jamaican servant, but she frightened his wife, made her uneasy. Sometimes, Naty associated the black woman with a large bread knife, held at an assassin's angle. At other times, in her dreams, the woman seemed less menacing, and danced around the bedroom wearing Doña Natica's blue dress, the one she'd worn to Naty and Orlando's wedding. When Orlando returned, he listened to his wife's complaints, and suffered her recriminations without really understanding her fears. Hoping to make things better, he promptly fired the servant.

Orlando was enchanted when their daughter, Nina, was born in 1949. In some sense, he had accepted that he bored his wife and that there wasn't much he could do about it. But this little girl delighted him, made him absolutely sing the praises of domestic life. His wife established a more remote connection to her daughter, leaving her, for the most part, in the care of a nanny. In later years, Naty would insist that a child always belongs to one parent or the other, and that Nina had always been Orlando's.

After the birth of her daughter, Naty went about constructing another world for herself. She distanced herself from people whose conformity bored her. It was exhilarating, the thought of a different, other life. With the benefit of hindsight, her friends would understand that Naty was leaving them behind because she was moving into a volatile political arena— a place more congenial to her romantic sensibility. Naty wanted a connection to a man who was a dreamer, a visionary, someone whose cause was noble. She couldn't imagine herself going to the barricades, but she could perfectly well see herself as the muse of a man who did.

. . .

Doña Natica, Naty, and Naty's firstborn, Nina, posing for a family portrait in 1949

ON MARCH 10, 1952, General Fulgencio Batista's coup d'état ended not just his own but also Fidel Castro's future career as a legitimate political figure. Castro had been running for Congress under Eddie Chibás's political banner, but the elections of June 1952 were canceled as soon as Batista seized power. In the 1930s, the Cubans had revered Batista as the young idealist who overthrew the government of the hated General Machado. In turn, Batista's torch would pass to Fidel, another promised redeemer who would turn himself into an angry tyrant.

Hugh Thomas, who dismisses Batista as a sort of "Caribbean confidence man," characterizes the coup as "an event comparable in the life of an individual to a nervous breakdown after years of chronic illness." At the time of this *golpe* that brought him to power, Havana had become an American wasteland presided over by Las Vegas mobsters. "Why not Cuba?" Meyer Lansky had said to Lucky Luciano, whom the government had banned from living in the United States. "You could operate from Havana the way you did in the old days."

Meyer Lansky had wanted to turn Havana into a more lucrative Las Vegas—a gamblers' paradise with casinos that stretched for miles along the edge of the sea. With General Batista's encouragement—his partnership with the Cuban dictator would cost the ambitious gangster millions of dollars—Lansky lured drug dealers, abortion extortionists, and high rollers to Havana. At his Hotel Capri, to welcome the gamblers, he even hired George Raft, Hollywood's favorite gangster—a man who came alive with the shuffle of the deck, the turn of the roulette wheel, the click of a prostitute's heels.

The Cubans despaired; they had turned to Eddie Chibás for deliverance at the next election. Just a few years before, Chibás had founded the Ortodoxo Party, whose endearing, innocent aim was the elimination of all corruption in government. On Sunday evenings, everyone was glued to the radio program in which Chibás crusaded against dishonest politicians. Naty adored him. She thought she'd found a man of noble thoughts, elevated sentiments, someone worthy of her complete devotion.

A small, portly man who wore thick lenses, a child of wealthy parents who'd given all his inherited money to the poor, Eddie Chibás was the most charismatic political figure of his time. One night in August 1951, he went on the air, encouraged the people to resist corruption, then shot himself in the stomach. He had accused the minister of education of stealing millions from the government treasury and hiding the money in Guatemala, but he couldn't produce the necessary evidence. Someone phoned Naty's house to say that Chibás had shot himself with a .38 Colt Special Revolver and was being rushed to Orlando's clinic. For three days, until he finally died, Naty maintained a vigil outside the fallen leader's room.

WE WERE sitting in the bar of the Hotel Nacional when Naty began to tell me the story of Fidel's attack on the garrison of Moncada. (Something about her attracts a bartender's curious glance: a Cuban woman, obviously so, but vital, not tired from the battles of the morning.) She started by recalling how everyone dressed during the decadent time of General Batista—how mannered everyone looked. In the winter, the men wore tweed jackets and gabardines, the women silver fox and stone marten; the casinos were filled every night. "I heard Eartha Kitt sing in this very room," she said. But suddenly she became distracted, stopping mid-sentence.

"On March 10, 1952," she told me, "we all dressed entirely in black. On the radio, I had heard the news that General

Batista had overthrown the government, suspended the Constitution, and established himself as the new dictator. The deposed Cuban president, Carlos Prío Socarrás, was granted political asylum in Mexico. There would be no elections in June, with their promise of decent government—Fidel Castro, for example, elected to a seat in Congress. When the United States immediately recognized the government of the military dictator, I felt even more terrible."

Naty Revuelta wasn't there when protesting student leaders congregated near the university to bury a facsimile of the Constitution. But she might as well have been. Her husband didn't like her wandering off in the evenings, stumbling into causes larger than their marriage. Having separated herself from her friends at the Biltmore Country Club, Naty was connecting, instead, to the radical students and their plans for reclaiming Cuba. "I went to a locksmith and had three keys made to my house," Naty explains. "I sent one to the head of the Ortodoxo Party, the second to their presidential candidate, and the third to Fidel. I heard immediately from the other two men—their gratitude was apparent—but not, of course, from Fidel."

Searching for someone who could incarnate her diffuse, inchoate, patriotic ideals, Naty was intrigued by the charismatic Castro. A 1950 graduate of the University of Havana, he had studied law and social sciences but hadn't even a remote interest in either discipline. His passion was for agitation, revolution; he would fight to rid his country of both General Batista and the Yankee imperialists.

"When I sent him the key to my house," Naty says, "I had met Fidel only once. After Batista's coup, I was introduced to him at a student demonstration, but then he went into hiding. Several months later, he sent a friend to my house to tell me that he needed my support. I learned that he had gone underground, in order to denounce General Batista from several clandestine radio stations. I never got to listen to his broadcasts, because the police found his hideout, confiscated the radio equipment, and that was the end of it."

NATY stares into the past. It's as though she dates herself from the moment when her life first intersected with Fidel's. She begins to tell her story. Once upon a time. . . . Her tone, formal and practiced, reminds me that she has told it often: "One afternoon—it must have been in January, or February, 1953—Fidel finally came to the house to see me. He explained that he was organizing his own revolutionary movement, because he couldn't support the opposition's commitment to passive resistance. General Batista's regime had come to power violently, and had to be removed in the same way. Fidel believed that Cubans had too much hot blood in them to wait for the results of a Gandhi-like position."

When Orlando came home from the clinic, he joined the discussion. "After listening to Fidel," Naty continues, "my husband put his hand in his pocket, drew out all the money he'd made that day—it must have been over a hundred dollars— and gave it to Fidel for his revolutionary activities. Orlando was opposed to General Batista, who had come like a thief, in the middle of the night. But more to the point, Fidel impressed him as a brave, trustworthy man."

Unconsciously, there was probably more to it. After all, a man who wishes to please his younger, restless wife might find it useful to contribute to any cause that has captured her interest. Naty, smitten with the young revolutionary, accompanied Fidel out of the house: "If you need me," she said, "please count on me."

"A few weeks later," Naty continued, "he began to use my house as a meeting place for the rebels. In that house—together with Abel Santamaría and Jesús Montane—Fidel Castro completed his plan to attack the Moncada garrison on the 26th of July."

W H O W A S this man whom Naty first met on the steps of the university? Some swear that Fidel Castro was a Communist when his mother rocked him in his cradle, and others that he was a romantic adventurer whom American foreign policy turned into a ruthless cold-war villain. Perhaps he was no more than a spoiled rich boy who had never had to confront reality. In Miami, he's thought of as a ruthless dictator; but on the streets of Havana, the crowds still cheer him. For this story, it's what Naty has made of him that's important.

As much as Naty insists upon a political justification for her revolutionary activities, it was her burgeoning passion for Fidel that cemented her devotion to his cause. She fastened onto him, turned all her attention towards him. However much she may have admired his politics, Naty spent months helping Fidel plan the attack on Moncada because she was falling in love with him.

"Happy love has no history," according to Denis de Rougement, in *Love in the Western World*. "Romance only comes into existence where love is fatal, frowned upon and doomed by life itself." Through passion, Naty understood, there is a connection to the infinite. For that reason, it doesn't seem to matter to lovers that passion—indifferent to moral structures, protective not even of itself—often leads to ruin.

With Fidel, Naty convinced herself she could experience life more intensely. But she also sensed that theirs was an ill-fated love. Both were married, but more than a legal barrier

Naty, 1953

separated them. From the moment she met him, Naty told me, she believed that Fidel would be killed in the struggle. That persistent fatalism heightened sensation, forged the deepening bond between them, turned, in fact, an *amistad amorosa* into a doomed romance.

Even today, long after the bitter end of revolutionary promise, Naty Revuelta softens when she remembers her excitement in the months before Fidel's attack on Moncada. Opposition to General Batista's coup, together with enthusiasm for Fidel, had brought together disgruntled students, political radicals, and frustrated idealists. It was Fidel's romantic plan—naïve, secret, dependent upon improbables—to overcome the army garrison at Moncada (as well as another, in Bayamo, eighty miles to the west), to secure its guns and ammunition, and, finally, to effect a spontaneous, popular uprising against Batista.

A wondrous city drenched in history—it was founded by Diego Velázquez and named for the "Slayer of the Moors"—Santiago had the advantage of being far from Havana and well known to Fidel, who had gone to boarding school there. He planned the raid for July 26 at 5:15 a.m., the morning after the last night of Carnival in Santiago. Fidel counted on nothing more threatening than a garrison of surprised, drunken soldiers, spent after an evening's carousing.

Once the garrison was taken, a manifesto would be read over a Santiago radio station, declaring the commitment of the revolutionaries to the patriotic ideals of José Martí and Eddie Chibás. A daring Naty offered to type the manifesto and distribute the copies throughout Havana. She also chose the music to be played before and after Fidel's words were read on the air: Beethoven's *Eroica*, selections from Prokofiev, Mahler, Dvořák, and Berlioz, and the Cuban national anthem.

As he was leaving for Santiago, on July 24, Fidel stopped at Naty's house to collect his copies of the manifesto and to give her his last-minute instructions for delivering the rest on the morning of the attack: "You mustn't leave the house before dawn on Sunday. That's the time of the attack. If you're caught before then, we'll be discovered before we're ready." And he added, "Please do what you can for the families of the men who are going with me. I wish I could do without them, but I can't." She noticed his seriousness, the creases in his white shirt.

A day before this meeting, Fidel had summoned Naty to the house of one of his followers. Never before had this usually remote man been so tender: "You know," he said, "it's going to be very hard for me to leave you. You have become so dear to me. I don't know what will become of us, but I want you to know that I am placing you on an altar inside my heart." "It was then," Naty tells me, "that I realized I was falling in love with him."

JULY 26, 1953. On Sunday morning, at three o'clock, there is no light. Naty Revuelta, tired from a sleepless night, rises from the bed she shares with her husband. Nina, their daughter, lies fast asleep in her room, her hand curled around a miniature rag doll. Even Tata, the child's vigilant nurse, has given in to the silence and the dark. Orlando, who had worked all evening in his clinic, hasn't stirred at all. But when Naty drops her hairbrush on the floor, he awakens and wonders where she's going at that hour. She mutters something about getting up to read and waits for him to pursue the matter. Orlando, exhaustion overwhelming him, turns onto his side and once again falls asleep. Naty puts on her clothes, lights a cigarette, and makes herself a thimbleful of black coffee. Until the sun rises, she paces around the garden, then gathers her documents, opens the front door, and steps into the Havana morning.

At a farmhouse in Siboney, just outside of Santiago, Fidel Castro puts on a fake Batistiano army uniform that is much too big for him. He gives last-minute commands to his fellow rebels, Jesús Montane and Abel Santamaría. Jesús, who worked for General Motors, had met Fidel two years before, when he arranged for Fidel to buy a car on credit. At the same time, Abel Santamaría was also working for GM, the Pontiac division. Neither man has had any military training.

With the men stand Melba Hernández, a young lawyer, and Haydée Santamaría, Abel's sister—the two women who have been training with them in Havana. When the uprising ends, both women, captured while attending the wounded, will be incarcerated for seven months at a women's prison outside of Havana. Haydée will have lost both her brother and her fiancé. Abel Santamaría, more optimistic than the others, hadn't foreseen that he and Jesús Montane would be killed. He planted some mangoes when he arrived at Siboney before the assault. "Just you wait," he said, "three years from now, you'll see how many of these mangoes I'm going to eat."

IT IS four-forty-five in the morning when about 160 untrained rebels, in twenty-six cars, leave for Moncada with a few shotguns, some hunting rifles, and a Thompson submachine gun. Fidel Castro has forgotten his glasses and finds it hard to see. About half the rebels, unfamiliar with Santiago's winding streets, lose their way and never even reach the garrison. Those that gain entrance find themselves looking for guns in the barbershop instead of the armory. Defeated by poor planning and the resistance of Batista's soldiers, Fidel Castro calls for an immediate retreat. About half of the guerrillas are captured and then tortured and killed; Fidel himself heads for the hills.

Naty Revuelta, meanwhile, doesn't know what's happening

in Santiago. She has a list of people to whom she's ready to deliver Fidel's manifesto: political figures, leaders of the opposition, the editors and publishers of *El Diario de la Marina, El Mundo, El País,* and even the *Havana Post.* She's proud of the document, with its commitment to the ideals of her adored José Martí. Around ten o'clock, when she reaches the house of the editor of *Prensa Libre,* she hears the news. The assault on Moncada has ended in failure, and the rebels who have survived the assault—those who aren't still hiding in the hills—have been arrested.

At the Vedado Parish Church, where she stops on her way home, Naty genuflects in front of the altar. She tells the priest in confession that she is there on behalf of her friends, who are in danger of death and may not have the opportunity to receive the sacrament. Together, they make the sign of the cross. *En el nombre del padre . . .* (In the name of the Father . . .) Naty believes the priest to be a humane man—someone who won't compromise her, place her in an awkward position—a belief that is reinforced when he freely gives her absolution and offers her Communion.

When Naty returns home, she is still numb. Orlando is listening to a radio broadcast that denounces the rebels, not as political insurgents, but as common criminals. (She doesn't hear the students accuse Fidel of cowardice, his own followers condemn him for leading young men to their certain death.) Naty's name is never mentioned. She believes that she'll be protected because she's married to a prominent doctor—no one wants to suggests that a privileged, establishment Cuban might support the rebel cause.

That afternoon, Orlando, Nina, and Naty leave their house, drive to the Biltmore, have lunch on the club's veranda, and spend the afternoon on the beach. When they return home, it is almost midnight. Even though he hasn't a clue about Naty's dramatic contribution to the event, Orlando feels uneasy, nervous. He hires a chauffeur to make sure that his wife and daughter will always have protection.

ON AUGUST 1, Lieutenant Pedro Manuel Sarría encounters Fidel Castro sound asleep in a mountain hut. A compassionate man, Lieutenant Sarría couldn't have imagined that he would alter history when he refused to allow his soldiers to shoot a failed insurrectionist and his scruffy companions. In the words of Castro's biographer Tad Szulc: "A corporal shouted to Sarría, 'Lieutenant, we'll kill them!' Sarría, a tall, black, fifty-three-year-old professional officer, raised his arm. 'No,' he roared, 'don't kill them! I order you not to kill them! I am in command here. . . . You can't kill ideas. . . .'"

Later, Lieutenant Sarría had Castro remanded to the civilian prison in Santiago. In refusing to take him to Moncada, where the military authorities would have tortured and shot him, Lieutenant Sarría saved Fidel's life for the second time in a single day. Serendipity? It occurs to me that, in every successful life, there's probably a generous measure of good fortune. A god intervenes, with a blessing. Destiny is arbitrary, out of one's control. That's what makes misfortune so unbearable.

At home in Havana, Naty senses danger. Among Fidel's few personal belongings, the authorities have found a note that Naty had given to him as he was leaving for Moncada. She strains to remember what she'd said. "I remember writing that I understood it was his duty to go with the rebels to Santiago. And I said that, whatever happened, I would always remember him." Was it a love note? Perhaps not, but it was filled with affection.

When Doña Natica hears that the authorities have confiscated Naty's letter to Fidel, she visits friends in Santiago to try to determine if her daughter is in danger. While she's there, someone suggests that she tell Naty to plead for political asylum in a foreign embassy. Rumors abound. Naty's name has been mentioned more than once. In Abel Santamaría's luggage, after his murder, the police find some books with her name written in them.

Later, Naty learns that her note, the one found in Fidel's pocket, has actually helped her. It leads the authorities to believe that Naty has a personal, not a political connection to Fidel. But Doña Natica's fears are not quieted. She worries so much about her daughter that her hair falls out in clumps.

In the Provisional Court in Santiago, after a secret trial, the judges sentence Fidel to fifteen years in the National Men's Prison on the Isle of Pines. "Condemn me," he says, "it does not matter. History will absolve me." (A Cuban writer exiled in Miami would later comment: "History may absolve him—but geography never will.")

After serving just over twenty months of their sentences, Fidel Castro and the other rebels are released from prison. Although he is only twenty-eight, Fidel's stature is already impressive. A nationwide campaign to secure unconditional amnesty for the Moncada prisoners—a campaign that Fidel abets from his cell—threatens the government's stability. With the fear that he might lose power, that the Fidelistas are gaining momentum as the Batistianos falter, General Batista grudgingly signs the amnesty bill on May 6, 1955. Suppose someone had told him that on January 1, 1959, he would climb into the DC-4 that would carry him into exile. How could he have known that nothing he did much mattered? At Moncada, the history-changing July 26 Movement was born.

CHAPTER 5

Naty and Fidel

NATY REVUELTA took a photograph of Felix de Cossío's painting—the portrait of herself in the green evening dress—and sent it to Fidel at the prison in the Isle of Pines. She pasted the print on some *papel alba* (the opaque white paper used by architects), made a cover of it for her secondhand edition of Somerset Maugham's *Cakes and Ale* (which both she and Fidel referred to as *Rosie*), and mailed the novel to him. "I didn't make a single mark on the book, nor did I enclose a letter with it. I wanted to be sure that the message would get through. Whatever the outcome of Moncada, I had promised to let Fidel know that, afterward, I was safe. I sent him *Rosie* to reassure him, but also to please him, because he loved the woman in the painting."

Who was this icon of female loveliness? Who was the woman with whom Fidel Castro was infatuated? Imagine the socialite in that portrait leaving Havana, following Fidel Castro from the Isle of Pines to Mexico, and then on to the Sierra Maestra—a flash of patterned silk, taffeta, and emeralds riding on a tank, hoisting a rifle over her shoulder.

·   ·   ·

NATY'S passion for Fidel brackets her period of revolutionary fervor, when she believed that everything was possible. Their letters reveal the contours of a liaison between two brave and formidable, if misguided, people in their late twenties: a political prisoner and a restless young woman. Enamored of Naty, Fidel remained connected to her until the fever passed; then he wanted nothing more to do with her. But Naty, who thought she had given her heart, refused to be discarded; she would live frozen in that moment in time, the moment in which Fidel had loved her.

When Naty first read to me from the letters, she asked: "This was the man I loved. What happened to him?" The young Fidel who writes to Naty bares his passion, his intelligence, his capacity to make the best use of adversity. But it's possible, in most of the letters, to see hints of the later Fidel: the self-discipline, the hardening of the will, which would give him as much protection as the Cuban armed forces.

In the earliest letters, the egocentric Fidel doesn't rise to the surface. With the advantage of hindsight, I can detect that self-regarding side in protests of love for Naty that seem not so much written to an individual woman as composed for posterity. Yet, while he was imprisoned on the Isle of Pines, Fidel gave few signs of the future dictator he would become.

There is something high-minded, as well as passionate, about both young people. "Natty, my first letter—the one with which we initiated this joyous correspondence—was very short, because I didn't have anything else to say. I was being honest and wasn't expecting anything in return, more like a debtor, not a creditor; I wasn't asking for anything, but, rather, offering myself entirely."

Naty delights in bringing her world to him. She makes sure that he has a Spanish translation of Rudyard Kipling's "If—," her favorite poem. She sends him a brilliantly colored kaleidoscope. "It made me so sad that he couldn't see the sunset, the sky, and the trees." She mails him concert programs, articles about writers and literature, about the new direction of Italian cinema.

It was an innocent time, an interlude.

FIDEL CASTRO knew how to make love to a woman without ever touching her. Naty Revuelta was a beauty, but Fidel didn't have to tell her so; that was for the men who flirted with her at the Vedado Tennis Club. Instead, he courted her with his intelligence—and his convictions. Fidel made her feel that he relished her lively mind, doted on her intuitive sensibilities. He never mentioned her fabulous green eyes.

They write to each other about Romain Rolland's *Jean Christophe*—a fashionable novel about a passionate young musician, a man whose genius is at the mercy of a rigid, uncompromising spirit. Rolland's hero scorns most other people, denounces the world as mediocre, and, finally, prefers to be alone. "Jean Christophe," Naty writes, "is a superior spiritual being." Naty and Fidel's comments on *Jean Christophe* concentrate on their shared admiration for the hero's existence on a higher plane—one that transcends the commonplace. "Rolland," Fidel writes to her, "belongs to the same ideological group as José Ingenieros, H. G. Wells, Maxim Gorki, and other novelists characterized by their yearning for justice."

When he was a very young man, Fidel had married Mirta Díaz-Balart, a country girl without the slightest interest in his plans for revolution. It's ironic that, on their honeymoon in New York, riding through the city in a rented white convertible, Fidel acquired his first copy of *Das Kapital*. Mirta wanted nothing more than a conventional marriage and the chance to

A very young and petulant Fidel Castro

raise her children in peace. She might, in fact, have been the ideal wife for Naty's Orlando.

According to one of Castro's biographers, Mirta was the only woman Fidel ever loved. I rather doubt it. Certainly, you couldn't reach that conclusion from the way he treated her. He seems to have given Mirta very little thought, using her as though she were a servant and he the young master. When he considered Mirta at all, Fidel assumed that either his relatives or their influential friends would take care of her.

In any case, domestic matters held no interest for him. When Mirta and Lidia, his sister, quarrel with each other, Fidel complains to Naty, "I have told Mirta that prison permits me to be content living apart from petty problems, it allows me that sweet peace. I'm going to write a letter to the tribunal reproaching them for having sentenced me to fifteen years rather than twenty."

No—Mirta was not for him. Naty Revuelta, the courageous sophisticate who had climbed out on a limb for Fidel during Moncada, was the right partner for the rebel who thought himself a hero. With Naty, Fidel could imagine reading about Simon Bolívar, discussing José Martí. "In each of my books," he writes to her, "you have a space on every page, in every phrase, in every word. I want to share with you every pleasure that I find in a book. Doesn't this mean that you are my intimate companion and that I am never alone?"

Cynics may protest that this was no more than Fidel's mating dance disguised as an intellectual bonding. But couldn't it have been both? When he writes to her, it's spontaneous, and with a lover's delight: "I received such pleasure from your last letter. Of course I like it! As always, you invent something new!" He continues: "Often, you make me laugh. It's as though I can hear you. You write with boundless charm and as though you were speaking to me. Into those letters, you put so much

ingenuity and style. I see your gestures and hear the sound of
your voice. Tell me: how do you know so many things?"

THE NOTION that Naty and Fidel have entered into the earliest stages of a love affair—a time when lovers aren't so much
real but of each other's making—is bolstered by Fidel's confidence in this invented woman. In Naty, he believes he's found
an imaginative partner—a lover of literature, of philosophy,
and of the arts, someone with no resemblance to his provincial
wife. More important, he's found a woman who will have no
trouble following him into the political thickets.

From Naty's point of view, Fidel is the ideal: brilliant, pure,
uncommon—a storybook hero uncompromising in his devo-
tions. She is struck by how different he is from her dutiful,
indifferent husband. When he praises her considerable talents,
she convinces herself that she is the very heroine he thinks her
to be. "You see people as they are," she writes, "and not as they
wish to be." His enormous pleasure in her must have been dis-
arming. "To think that I make you laugh, that you consider me
witty and full of grace (like the Hail Mary?). This has been my
selfish intention; it provides me with the greatest of rewards."

Naty's energy, her all-embracing curiosity about life, draws
him further into her private world. ("I'm overwhelmed," he
writes, "with a desire to know the works of all authors, the doctrines of all philosophers, the treatises of all economists, the
sermons of all apostles.") He tells her that he's reading Thack-
eray's *Vanity Fair,* Marx's *Das Kapital,* Turgenev's *A Nest of
Gentlefolk,* Maugham's *The Razor's Edge,* Villaverde's *Cecilia
Valdés,* A. J. Cronin's *The Citadel,* etc., etc., etc.

Isolation, adversity, imprisonment. The harsh conditions
and his outlaw status bring out Fidel's most consistent trait: his
talent for self-reliance, his capacity to turn misfortune into

opportunity. "I'm immersed in books. . . . The hours pass like seconds. . . . I stop reading only to do the things that I've imposed on myself and my companions: two classes each day, and an hour of collective reading." He plans for a brilliant future when it is uncertain whether he will have a future at all.

Together, Fidel promises Naty, they can take on the world. "Are you interested?" He outlines a plan: "We'll study everything in a methodical, practical fashion. Carefully, calmly, I'll select the best works of Spanish, French, and Russian literature. You do the same with English literature. I'll take care of the arid, dense areas of government, economics, and social doctrine. . . . You'll be in charge of music. . . . Do you like the idea? I have fifteen years, more than enough time, in which to do this."

In one of her first letters to Fidel, Naty wrote: "I'd like to be more than I am. . . . Can you help me? Put my thoughts in order." Now her intellectual mentor, Fidel is bent on transforming her into a more cultivated, sentient woman. "What do you think of the study plan I proposed in my previous letter? I'll begin to work on it as soon as I receive word from you."

Naty answers: "I gladly accept your offer. I have the same time available as you do. I'll be responsible for English literature. The mere fact of having a plan makes me feel better. Don't forget to tell me if you can read in English. So much is lost in translation."

THEIR hidden world contains unprecedented excitement. But even then there are hints that their temperaments aren't entirely compatible. It is simply not in Naty's nature to ignore the lively material world. (One day, it will be her fate to have to choose between the revolutionary and the bourgeois—but that's later.) She is more intent on celebrating Christmas than in reading Kant and Hegel. She may not have known it then, but she would find her freedom in the shifting spaces between both worlds.

For her daughter, Naty writes, she has found a doll with skates; for the orphanage of San Vicente, she has decorated a tree. "For the Feast of the Three Kings, I bought your son [Fidelito] a car that has lights and runs on batteries. I also bought him a box of lead Cowboys and Indians [and] a pair of so-called 'skijamas.' . . . I tried to find a pair for you so that you could have similar ones, but I couldn't find any." Who could have foreseen then that Fidel would cancel Christmas when he came to power?

Worlds impinge. In her office at Esso Standard Oil, it is well known that Naty is a fanatic about Fidel Castro. When there are confidential financial reports to file, someone else is asked to handle them, because Naty's superiors consider her too much of a revolutionary to be trusted. In the next few years, like a drill sergeant, Naty will encourage her female colleagues to practice marching in the office corridors. (Cuban women aren't good at it, Naty confesses later, because they just can't take the sway out of their hips.)

Between both worlds, she moves with ease. "I was disappointed that I couldn't write to you yesterday," she admits. "I had to take my boss to the airport and pick up my mother, who was away for a month following in the footsteps of the Queen of England. She has returned with endless stories, even new gossip about the royal family. . . ."

FIDEL CASTRO is smitten. He delighted even in their first lovers' quarrel. Why should other people get so many letters from him, Naty has complained? When she's angry, Fidel writes back, Naty reminds him of a "raging storm," and of "spectacular lightning." "What do the letters I write to the rest of the world, their number, or the time I spend on them have to do with those I write to you? How can you doubt that so many of my thoughts dwell in a special place that belongs to you? The part of you which belongs to me accompanies me always, and it will be so forever. Does one who can't find the words to express his affection merit such little kindness?"

It was intriguing. I hadn't seen the letter that prompted that tender response from Fidel. Naty had never shown it to me. This had to do with her pride—she couldn't reveal that she had been needy, couldn't allow me to see that she had lost her control. It's not hard to imagine that, whenever Fidel's attention turned somewhere else, even for a moment, she thought she'd been deserted.

To calm her down, Fidel teases her: "If we depended on you for world peace, there would be war." And then he writes: "I want your letters as much as you want mine. But perhaps I need them even more. Why must you say: 'I do not know how to love when I am not loved'?" Most significantly, she still excites him: "As for the rest, Natty, your letter is a true waterfall, a torrent which pours through the floodgates and overflows. It amazes me. On three sheets of paper, there are a hundred pages of ideas. Are you always like this when you're angry? What a formidable ability to synthesize!"

Mollified, Naty answers: "That lightning which you saw on the horizon was not directed at you, or at anyone else. I have it inside myself, and if you see it, it's because you know about it. No one else can imagine it. What power to synthesize? Well, I'd like to know how to concentrate on one subject, only one, develop it, and write to you about it ad nauseam." Her attachment to him, the desire for adulation to confirm her self-worth, has become stronger. "Who else in the world knows me better than you?" she writes. "Since I started writing, I don't keep any secrets. My soul is open to you."

The Cubans would have said that Naty was *candelada*—a moth at the flame.

FRIGHTENED when the earth tremors, when the tectonic plates shift, Naty constantly searches for balance. She regains her footing by abdicating personal responsibility for her plight. "You understand me, love me, need me the most," she writes to Fidel, "and I understand you the best. Who is to blame, after all, if God creates two people who are like each other and puts them in the same place at the same time?" If fate had placed her on the fault lines, how could she avoid the earthquake?

Curiously, Naty doesn't mention passion. She won't even admit that her feelings for Fidel have created a problem for her. Refusing to be hostage to a mythology of woman's unfaithfulness, she hijacks her own story, recasting herself as a madonna—a woman with a heart large enough to embrace everyone. "If I'm good because I love you [Fidel] it must mean that I'm unjust to Ando [her husband], Tatín [her daughter], and Mother. How can I explain that there's room for all four of you in my heart and that I'd rather die before hurting any of you?"

It's quite true. It is in the same maternal role in which Naty seeks to protect her household that she tries to control Fidel's behavior. "Cover up during these hot and cold days. Don't do anything mad. Take care of your teeth so that, when you read my letters, there's a white smile on your face. Remember that nicotine stains the teeth and that you smoke like a chimney." "Did you smoke the cigars that she [Mirta] gave you?" Naty tells him what to do, invades every part of his life. "Write to me. Don't tell me that you'll write and then not do it. That's a privilege that I reserve for myself. . . ."

Fidel remains, through all of this, infatuated. He writes: "My convictions are reaffirmed each time I read your letters. Nature has been much more than generous in endowing you with spirit and intelligence without forgetting to lavish attention on your nonspiritual side." And later: "I repeat that I cannot be forgiven for having asked you to write to me so much. I should have remembered that you have many obligations. Although I have these faults, you know that the one who writes always remembers and loves you. . . ."

FIDEL inhabits a different dimension. Naty has written that they are both captives. "Aren't we all in a prison?" But a housewife's gilded cage bears no resemblance to a prisoner's grim cell. Incarceration has a profound impact on the once sociable Fidel. "I've become introverted . . . trying to live in this separate prison world so different from the almost imaginary world which we've left behind. . . . The path from one to the other . . . is filled with sacrifice and pain." For the first time, he listens to music, thinks about it. "This very moment I'm listening to the radio and hearing 'The Siege of Zaragoza.' What beautiful music . . . ! My blood boils. Could it be that one of my ancestors fought there?"

I suppose that isolation and loneliness were Fidel's only partners until he retreated into a world of ideas. After Moncada, and the months of solitary confinement, only the written word had meaning for him. Later, he would write that he was becoming a stranger to the ordinary world. "Circumstances separate me from this world," he tells Naty; "it no longer has a reality for me but takes, instead, the form of a dream."

Even his son doesn't matter to him until he sees his own reflection in the child. "Fidelito was a dear. He was much more affectionate than when he used to see me every day. Above all, he's a very sensitive and sensible child. Those who died [at Moncada] loved him dearly and he remembers all of them. One day he asked me: 'Papá, whatever happened to Gildo?' When I told him that he was in heaven, he started to weep inconsolably. I wasn't aware until then that he could understand death. . . . Since then, I've loved him even more because he's suffered as a result of what I believe in."

Fidel has the narcissist's disease—the unshaken confidence that attention should be centered on him. He never looks at other people, just seems to do so. He may pretend to understand the limitations on Naty's time, but there's a growing frustration on his part—the beginnings of anger. Three months after the letters commence, he complains about his negative feelings, apologizes for them, but he's not getting enough attention, and darker thoughts are invading: "At my side, I have an angel who's always defending you: he tells me that I have ten times the amount of time to write that you have . . . that one tender, noble letter of yours is worth more than three of mine."

In that angel's admonishing voice, Fidel describes Naty as he wants to see her: "She exhausts herself running around searching for the books you want. . . . Do you think she hasn't suffered enough for you . . . ? You wanted a photograph of her and she sent it. Afterward, you earnestly wondered if she photographed herself in order to please you or if it was a pure coincidence; was her sweet look for you or just a coincidence . . . ?" But he can't hide his irritation. Fidel is restless, his fingers beginning to tap on the bars of his cell.

. . .

STILL, the fairy tale has a bit longer to run; no one has released Fidel into the active world. "Perhaps the world has forgotten me, couldn't care less about me. . . . For the moment, I've forgotten it. Do you know that I can count those I write to on my fingers? . . . That's how I measure the great affection I have for you, that is, by how I've forgotten the rest of the world." He signs the letter: "I love you very much. Fidel."

In her answer, Naty's voice is affectionate, carefree. She's neglected him and is glad that he's miffed. After all, the two have claims on each other. "Dear Fidel, The good angel whom you mention has not only defended me but, being angelical, has brought me your letter. . . . I believe the angel has lashed out at you too harshly. I'm going to ask him not to defend me so much but, always, to remain at your side. Once again, your letter calms me. You always manage it."

Naty can afford to be generous. Fidel's letter, with its demand for her attention, has made her aware of the power she has over him. She relishes this private, amorous Fidel, whom she needn't share with the rest of the world. It's a measure of a new sense of security that she can laugh at her bossiness: "I would also like it, Fidel, if you didn't neglect to study law. Do you have a subscription to a publication in that field? Wouldn't it benefit you . . . ? Soon you'll be saying: Yes, Mom. No, Mom. . . ."

When Naty writes to Fidel in early February 1954, they are still in the process of discovering each other. Separation has spared them the onset of boredom. Their letters are charming, even playful. They trade anecdotes. Naty tells him about her childhood. She had loved eating sweet dough at her neighbor's house each afternoon and had spent a good deal of her time "looking at multicolored fish in a garden pond." Fidel replies that a teacher once punished him by having him kneel on kernels of corn while carrying weights in his hands.

In this vein, Naty rambles on: "Do you know that this is the first time in my life that I want to study and to learn? . . . I used to wear my school uniform with a hat, because I developed a skin problem and my head had to be shaved. I would not allow anyone to see me. I would bathe and sleep with my hat on. I remember that it was light-blue with yellow flowers and a black border. I felt miserable and became very thin. The doctor prescribed lots of sun, so I was taken to the beach. I assure you that I looked ridiculous wearing swimming trunks and that hat! . . ."

But the letter takes a significant turn. The child in the hat with the yellow flowers, the young girl, grows serious. Offered a chance to transcend a small world, Naty speaks of a larger, altruistic life: "If I were alone and had the money . . . I would have a children's nursery in my garden rather than a greenhouse. It would offer medical services. Every four years, I would accept ten to twenty Cuban infants whose mothers had to work for a living. I would provide them with proper nutrition and health care until they were old enough to go to school. The tragedy of poor children is that the odds are against them from the time of their births."

(In American Cuba, the land of Del Monte and Libby's canned fruits and vegetables, the stockpile was so enormous that it would last the Cubans almost through the 1960s. But before the revolution, nothing was available to the poor.) It's not hard to dismiss Naty's childlike fantasy of saving the children. But give her credit for having a passion for a better Cuba; give her credit for avoiding complacency. Restless, eager, Naty also wants a private world. "Fidel," she writes in closing, "when is the first spaceship leaving for Mars?"

11

ON FEBRUARY 12, 1954, Colonel Ramos, known as Pistolita (the Little Gunman), came to the prison hospital ward where Fidel Castro and the other Moncada rebels had been assembled to tell them that they would be confined to their cells that day. General Batista had arrived on the Isle of Pines to inaugurate a power plant; his entourage would pass right by the prison, under their noses. Fidel Castro couldn't resist encouraging his men to burst into a patriotic song for the occasion. "Forward, all Cubans, may Cuba ever prize our heroism. . . ."

When the general heard the prisoners singing the freedom march composed for Moncada, he was furious. In retaliation, Fidel was placed in solitary confinement, where he would remain (Raúl, his brother, joined him after six months) until he was released in the general amnesty granted to all political prisoners fourteen months later.

Melba Hernández and Haydée Santamaría, on the other hand, were released from the women's prison, and resumed their activities on behalf of Fidel. Soon Fidel would look outside, past Naty Revuelta and into a future crowded with his followers. He would not see her. But for now, the letters between them became more intimate.

Isle of Pines
February 27, 1954

My dearest Natty,

. . . I don't like hearing that your letters are short because you're so busy. False, false! It seems like a cruel revenge against me. To my even greater mortification, you hide behind such fine pretexts. But what's making me suffer the most at this moment is that I really *must* be brief. Earlier, when I lay down, I fell asleep. Now it's late and they'll be collecting the mail soon, so there isn't time to be tender in these few lines. They may make you feel as though someone had thrown a bucket of ice water on you. . . .

I no longer have newspapers, magazines, a radio, nor do I have anyone to whom I can talk. Although I have fewer things to do and I don't waste any time, the hours still seem to run out. I have never seen time pass at such incredible speed. People in history, characters in novels, and the ideas of the greatest philosophers provide me with good, useful, unforgettable company.

Since I don't live in the present and can't get any information from the world, I'm living in other times that I find just as interesting, if not more so. Each era has had its moments, and history presents them to us—clean of impurities, excluding small things, gathering the most important events, the best philosophy, art, and science. I stroll among them holding hands with my imagination. In certain instances, I feel incredibly free and happy. This is my life now.

They have just arrived to collect the mail. I have asked for a minute. At least I've had the envelope ready.

I send you a quick hug,
Fidel

To stage a revolution, to rule Cuba, was not beyond Fidel's ambitions, which makes his patience remarkable. He doesn't fret offstage, waiting for his entrance. He seems the heir to the throne, in no particular hurry to take the crown and scepter, sure of his future.

Isle of Pines
March 1, 1954

My dearest Natty,

I'm going to count the days that you don't write to me. Remember that I'm now alone and will count each day as two. What would you say if I concluded that you have completely forgotten me?

For the past fifteen days I've been living in a solitary cell. There's absolute peace, but after six-thirty, because there's no more natural light, I have to dedicate my time to thinking. I don't have any other source of light. Sometimes I make a lamp, using matches and oil. Although I get good results, everything is stained. I feel terrible not being able to write at night, because it's when I have the most inspiration.

In spite of everything, I read often. That's how I spend my time. I feel lazy about writing, but that has an explanation. In trying to deal with loneliness, I've had to remake myself. I can't get disheartened, and must maintain my spiritual balance. . . .

These past days, many books have gone through my hands. I have developed a certain preference for Dostoevsky's novels. He is, without a doubt, the most formidable Russian writer. . . . Karl Marx liked [Balzac's] works and I can see why. . . . I can't begin to tell you how enthusiastic I've been about Victor Hugo's *Les Miserables*. But as time passes by, I am getting a bit tired of his excessive romanticism, his pomposity, and the sometimes tedious, immense weight of his erudition. Where Hugo can see only a contented adventurer, Marx sees the inevitable results of the social contradictions and the prevailing conflicts of interest. For some, history is good fortune, for others, it is a process ruled by laws. Hugo's statements, which remind me of our own discussions, are full of poetic faith. . . .

I must also speak to you about Freud. I have four volumes of his complete works and I expect the rest soon: a total of eighteen. . . . I plan to connect his insights to Dostoevsky's—a writer whose characters reveal his understanding of the subconscious.

However, I'm focusing most of my attention in another direction. I've rolled up my sleeves and have undertaken the study of world history and political doctrines. Given what I'm already covering, it may seem an excessive task and somewhat disorganized, but I can assure you that I'm keeping a rigorous schedule. I started with antiquity and, not satisfied with the reductive historical exposition I received from one formidable book, I'm referring to original works as much as possible within my unfortunately limited bibliographical resources. Since I'm moving along with great speed, making great strides, I feel very satisfied and in high spirits.

I must reproach myself for having written almost entirely about my own activities. Avenge yourself by writing as much as you can about yourself. I'll write soon.

I love you.
Fidel

March 3–5, 1954
Wednesday, 12 noon

My dearest Fidel,

You wonder what I would say if I thought you believed that I'd completely forgotten you. Well, I would say that, when you accuse me of forgetting, you are being unforgivably unjust. For example, now I'm always aware of nightfall. When there isn't any more light, I also start to wander about in the semidarkness. When you mention books, I run to get them so that I can write down the quotations you've chosen or elaborate on your thoughts about them. They are always interesting and enlightening. In them, I can sometimes imagine your sadness and, therefore, experience it as well. Every now and then, I laugh wholeheartedly about some witty phrase, feeling that you are well (of course, within reason), yet there are times when I get an uncontrollable urge to cry and wonder if it's because something is happening to you.

Do you understand? If I were your identical or Siamese twin, I wouldn't feel your sadness as close to me as I do. For it is also my own. For posterity's sake, let me add that my "confessions" to you (What a scandal!) are the result of an exceptional situation. Under normal conditions I'm a young woman like any other, capable of modesty, and of keeping her feelings to herself.

I also wanted to tell you that I have the small Napoleon by [Victor] Hugo. The temptation to be undisciplined is terrible when there are so many interesting books.

> I never forget you,
> Natty

Neither mentions the future. Naty tries to move past her conventional impulses in order to reach Fidel. She admits in her next letter (March 16, 1954) that she has been a conformist, worried about appearances. ("Do you know that it's a great struggle to free myself from these ties even though I despise them?") The prison bars that confine Fidel allow Naty her freedom to be intimate. Within this frame, she can bare her feel-

ings: "You're the single person with whom I completely iden-
tify and with whom I feel free to speak my mind. I can tell you
what I'm thinking and I accept your suggestions as if they were
second nature to me. If I don't act on them more openly, it's
due to unfortunate social conventions, a respect for appearances."

Almost in embarrassment, Naty changes tone when she
resumes writing on the following day. Once more, she's in control. "Don't strain your eyes so much that we we'll have to
send an eye doctor to you. I'm serious. Reading in dim light can
cause irreparable damage. I'm impatient (as you should be!) to
know whether you're exercising again and getting some sun."
Curiously, after she has confessed her need for Fidel, Naty
reasserts herself as a woman of strength: "Remember that a
modern woman is writing to you: a 'femme terrible,' a product
of the atomic era, of the industrial revolution, a woman from
an awkward generation, who, in order to maintain a certain
amount of economic freedom, paradoxically submits herself to
the slavery of an office desk. Who can understand us? Distance
is your savior!"

FIDEL'S response to Naty (March 22, 1954) compares the
pleasure he receives from the packages of books to that of children on the Feast of the Magi when they look underneath their
beds for their presents. He thinks back on his childhood. "We
would give our love to whoever fed our imaginations. 'Do you
know how to tell stories?' It was the first thing I'd ask anyone
who wanted to be my friend."

Reminding her of his solitary confinement, he tells her how
much he feels treated as though he were nothing more than a
barn animal and could not read. "I now have light. I didn't have
it for forty days and I learned to appreciate its value. I will

never forget it, just as I will never forget the seething humiliation of sitting alone in the shadows. Using a small, flickering oil lamp, I fought against their snatching away almost two hundred hours of light. My eyes were burning, my heart bleeding from indignation. Of all human cruelty, the least that I understand is that which is absurd. . . . After kissing all the books, I counted and saw that I had an extra kiss. With that kiss, I remember you."

April 19
Monday, 12 noon

My dearest Fidel,

On Thursday afternoon, I went to the embassy to browse around the library. I asked one of the employees to recommend a bibliography on the subject of Roosevelt's New Deal. He finally gave me a history of the United States and asked me not to tell anyone that he had given it to me—it's for distribution to organizations, not for individuals. He said: "You can have the book. It contains about forty pages on that 'jerk.'" (Look the word up in the dictionary.) "Right now we are trying to undo everything that [Roosevelt] did ten years ago."

Since he was so disrespectful, I finished his sentence: "And in ten years' time, somebody will be trying to undo everything you're doing now!" Can you imagine? Someone asks him about Roosevelt, and the first thing that he does is call him a "jerk," indirectly telling me that I'm a "jerk" since I'm the person who's interested in him! A newspaper reporter who works there was choking with laughter. "I'm not laughing," he said, "because of how you answered him. I'm laughing because you were able to get the book from him." Victory by exhaustion.

I forgot to tell you that I was able to get two copies,

one for each of us. It is entitled *A Brief History of the United States: The Biography of a Free Society*. One thing makes me indignant: when they speak of Cuba, [Carlos] Finlay isn't mentioned and yet [Walter] Reed is. Why, when Walter Reed has been recognized for his accomplishments, would anyone deny Carlos Finlay the credit to which he's entitled? I don't understand.

As far as you're concerned, I know I don't have to say it, but study often. If it's your fate to accomplish something, assure yourself that everything you do will proceed from love, understanding, or forgiveness of your fellow man. You cannot expect gratitude or compensation. I'm not being dramatic or ridiculously dogmatic. It's common sense. Everything else is destructive. Oh, Fidel, how I wish I were powerful enough to assist you, cultured in order to teach you, solid as armor in order to protect you!

Within this single letter, Naty challenges Fidel to make something of himself, lectures him on women, and mentions spending time with Mirta. Mirta remains an enigma—a woman not seen but dismissed. Another image of Naty and Fidel will surface: a couple living in mirrors, their self-regard, their failure to see Mirta as separate from themselves. Isn't she entitled to honesty, loyalty? And the emptiness from which this narcissism comes, isn't it in so many of these letters?

5:30 p.m.

I have gone out with Mirta twice. It's been such a great pleasure that I would like to have done it more often. She always has stories to tell—and this, despite her inevitable, involuntary reservations about me. Who can blame her? She is sweet and caring and never, at least to me, has she said anything that might be offensive. If it were any different, you know that I would tell you. Or maybe I would keep it to myself.

I finally gave in to summer. Last Saturday, I went to El Encanto and ordered an elegant dress to be made out of some silk I discovered abandoned at the bottom of a bureau drawer.

Women are flattered when there's an audience for all the stories they want to tell—some less interesting than others. If you don't want to create a distance between yourself and the woman in your life, pay attention to what she has to say. If you show her half the interest that she takes in your life, she'll never feel alone. Despite the distance, you are very good company.

> I love you,
> Natacha

> Isle of Pines
> April 27, 1954

My Dearest Natty,

. . . My letters are short these days. I don't write more than a page to anyone. You're the exception, so I'll write two pages. I haven't forgotten you. I'm entirely submerged in my thoughts, and when I leave them to write a letter, I want to finish it in two seconds. . . .

You write that you've sent me some candies and caramels. Well, I'm certainly going to be sweetened. In my thoughts, I always send you candies and caramels, too.

I'm very calm, peaceful. Perhaps now, in the near future, when I finish the last of the books I'm reading, I'll turn to a study of Cuba. I want to have, at the tip of my fingers, everything that there is to know about her, the paradise that can be made of her. I ponder these issues, reflect upon them. I feel pleasure in her reality, in the possibilities in store for her. More than ever, I love her [Cuba] like a suitor who follows a woman blindly without caring about the obstacles.

Your last letter is very interesting, like all of them. Always, they have the same effect on me. I receive them with the same pleasure and long for them with the same sadness. The last one moves me just as much as the first.

Will you worry less if you know that I'm content in spite of having spent 75 days in solitary confinement?

I love you,
Fidel

In May, Naty and Fidel's carefully constructed private world crumbles in a scenario that might have come from a popular *"telenovela."* What else could have condemned them to so banal a finale? Fidel had written to Naty, but someone sent the letter to Mirta instead. A few days later, Naty received the letter that had been intended for Mirta. ("My dearest Fidel," Naty wrote on May 5, "I am returning a letter which I presume isn't for me.")

In Havana, even today, people place the blame on an unnamed member of Mirta's pro-Batista family—a man with very good prison connections who could have had the letters switched before they were mailed from the Isle of Pines. Why not end Mirta's marriage to an irresponsible, difficult man who neither loved her nor had any intention of supporting her?

The evidence is only circumstantial; the switch of letters might have been entirely accidental. Whatever the source of this farcical mix-up, however, anger, rage, and humiliation were to follow. Mirta was twisting and turning; she would not forgive her husband. Naty, too, felt the winds of an approaching hurricane. If Fidel's marriage came crashing down, the breakup of her own household would follow. Though a Cuban marriage often survived a man's infidelity, it never recovered from the unfaithfulness of a woman. The world she'd created with Fidel rested on two very shaky triangles.

When Naty writes to Fidel about the mix-up, she's concerned with the damage. She urges Fidel to be "kind and tender" to Mirta. "If you haven't written [such a letter to her] do so now so as to erase some of her bitterness as well as the sadness that I feel inside myself. Please do this for me."

Contemplating her own future, though, terrifies Naty. She resists change, as though it will bring only abandonment and destruction. "I ask one thing of you: *Don't change towards her* [Mirta]. Be assured that I'll never change." In her panic, she is still able to soothe herself with the naïve idea that everything will be fine in the end. She takes on the tone of a schoolmistress: "Don't worry, everything in life has a solution. I hope that, as time goes on and you make it clear to her that you care, she'll realize that she's been unjust. I depend on you to correct the wrongful, hurtful interpretation she's made of me."

I suspect that Naty's hands trembled when she held Fidel's letter intended for Mirta. To Fidel, she claims that she hasn't opened it—although she must have read the salutation to Mirta—and adds that she has decided against sending it to Mirta: "I won't give it to her [Mirta], because if your letter to me was longer or more loving, it could make her angrier."

Defensive and anxious, Naty coaches Fidel: "Remember that [Mirta's] pride is hurt, that she's defending what belongs to her. Don't worry about me. My conscience is clear. The truth will eventually be known. Everything depends upon our being patient, and remaining calm."

. . .

N A T Y steadies her nerves by writing, and her letter to Fidel the following afternoon restores her poise. There she sits, fiddling with sentences, discarding one thought, replacing it with another, searching for an encouraging image of herself. Fidel has given her the attention, the self-esteem that she craved, but now she has trouble explaining, even to herself, that she is a woman of virtue. "Fidel, who else can I reach out to with the uncertainty that seizes me? I need you very much. Only one thing saddens me. In my desire to come to your aid, to understand you, where have my feelings taken me? I wanted to be a friend who could share your misfortune with you. I thought that, in some small manner, it would compensate for your sadness. I didn't imagine going beyond acceptable limits; my expectations were modest. I wanted to give happiness, not take it from someone. I don't understand how others have thought those feelings to be something so ugly, and harmful."

Not surprisingly, Mirta—a woman whose husband has neglected her and who has experienced his politics only as abandonment of her—unleashes her rage on the conventional "other woman." By blaming Naty for the failure of her marriage, Mirta makes sense of her misery. She promises to create a scandal unless Naty ceases to write to Fidel. Naty confides her worries to him: "[Mirta] feels hurt, wants to fight for her cause. [She] will take her revenge on me if I write to you again. I don't know what else she's thinking, or what she plans to do, but I feel uneasy. I never imagined such an unpleasant outcome."

Treating Mirta like an erupting volcano, Naty gives Fidel a lesson on how to manipulate his wife's feelings. "Act as though you hadn't heard from me. If a thousand women follow a man, his wife will forgive him as long as he has ignored them. But if the man praises even the most insignificant of the women, all his wife's anger will be unleashed. Don't defend me. Only the thought that your love for her hasn't changed will be able to satisfy her." Tossed around, desperate to recover the past, Naty seems to have no awareness of her own dishonesty towards Mirta. Cruel, perhaps, but very human, too—the need to have what one wants, the need to distort the mirror in one's own self-interest.

Where are they now? Fidel's in jail; Naty's safely at home. Fussing, like an oversolicitous mother with her child, Naty turns to other things: "I wasn't able to send you the medication. But I have it here. They're small, shiny red oval pills. Take them as soon as you get them. This is also an order. The symptoms of vitamin deficiency are terribly alarming."

Stumbling around, unaware that she's losing him, Naty strains, closing her letter of May 6 with melodramatic phrases: "I will now retreat into silence—one in which there is no forgetting. For those who know only how to act with their hearts, it's difficult to be reasonable. Whatever happens now depends upon you. The bitterness of life won't change me. God willing, the one who never forgets you always continues to be, Natacha."

Fidel focuses on the incident, but not for long. He writes two letters to Naty—one on May 7, another a week later—in which he apologizes for the pain he has caused her. He's mortified, humiliated, at the mercy of enemies who want to increase his sense of isolation. He isn't surprised about the letter switch; he considers it to have been deliberate, an instance of the outrageous treatment that any prisoner experiences. "I only regret forgetting that a political prisoner who maintains his dignity, who won't plead with the authorities, whose attitude is a burning rebuke to his enemies, will be treated in the vilest of manners."

The prison censor, whom Fidel trusts, has discovered that the switched letters, without being shown to him first, were both smuggled out of the prison. "Without going into detail," Fidel writes, "it's sufficient to tell you that I can explain everything, given what I know about the prison, who runs it, and how they do it."

Having said that, Fidel has finished. The past recedes, because it's no longer useful to him. He sets new terms for Naty, his voice grave, his tone much more formal. "I no longer confide in the mail. And so we must stop writing to each other. I don't have to add any explanations: I hope you continue to maintain the faith in me that you have professed so often. When I need something, I'll write a few short sentences on a piece of paper and send it to you, edited, so that nothing can be used for an ignominious end."

The clues are there. "You know," Fidel continues, "that personal matters are the least important to me." But, as though she were alone on the high wire, losing her balance, Naty is unable to recover her footing. Frightened, anxious, she doesn't understand that she has been dismissed.

"Don't worry about me: I'm fine. In the letter that never reached you, I thanked you for the last books you sent. In this one, I thank you not only for them but for all the other books. I'm so grateful for all that you have done for me. Is it possible that in return I have offered you nothing more than suffering and sorrow?"

IN JULY 1954, Mirta asked Fidel for a divorce. The Ministry of the Interior had just announced that she was losing her government sinecure—a *botella*, an unearned wage paid to those well connected to a political regime. Fidel heard about it on the radio in his cell and couldn't believe that his wife had been collecting money from Batista's government. A few days later,

Lidia visited him in prison to tell him that Mirta's brother had arranged for her *botella*. Fidel had made no provision for Mirta, none for his son. What did he expect her to do?

Naty claims to have forgotten much of what happened in the months that followed the scandal. Tennis, dances, lunch at Orlando's mother's house, an evening at a gambling casino, an occasional discreet letter sent to Fidel through his sister. After the infamous mail switch, he'd written Naty several letters, but they were impersonal, addressed to Lidia in case they were ever confiscated.

The affectionate play, the intimacy of the earlier correspondence, had vanished. Having moved on, Fidel wasn't interested in writing to Naty anymore. Partly, he hated domestic problems and scandals. But more to the point, he had become preoccupied with his role as the next Cuban savior. On December 13, 1954, he writes her: "For a while now, I've had the desire to learn more about our past, our people, the men who shaped our history. . . . There are plenty of men now here who are capable of making this island the most prosperous country in the world."

Probably Fidel wasn't even aware yet that Naty's attraction for him depended upon her being a conduit, a courier for him—granted, an exciting, desirable one. Fidel was using her to get the books he wanted; that's what remained of his passion. In the same letter, he writes: "I'll probably have to write again with a small list of books. Those I have here would be sufficient if I weren't so desperate to get others. I swear it's not a whim. These are the inconveniences of not having a public library at hand." At the end of the month, she answers: "When I read an article that's interesting, I'll send it to you without any explanation. I should end this letter now. Despite the immense pleasure and happiness it gives me [to write], I won't risk antagonizing you with my thoughts on matters about which I know so very little."

MAY 1955. At four o'clock in the morning, Naty leaves her bedroom secretly, careful not to awaken Orlando and Nina. She dresses and moves quietly towards the door, her red ballerina skirt and white off-the-shoulder blouse setting off her small waist and her golden tan. In her husband's Mercedes-Benz—Orlando always had the chauffeur polish the green car until it gleamed—Naty drives towards Batabanó, south of Havana, to join the crowds greeting Fidel, upon his release from prison. From the scrubby Isle of Pines (a place her grandfather once told her might be Robert Louis Stevenson's Treasure Island), he is traveling to the mainland by ferry.

Naty hasn't informed Orlando that she's going; it would only irritate him. In her marriage lately, everything seems to have become a problem. She can sense her mother-in-law's disapproval when she looks bored at the dinner table. But she just doesn't want to enter into the chatter about the seamstress, the carelessness of the maid. She'd rather be alone to dream of Fidel.

A scene from a movie. Naty arrives in Batabanó and catches a glimpse of Fidel surrounded by photographers, infatuated students, and hard-core political supporters. Cameras flash at a press conference on the ferry. He promises revolution. Sisters Lidia, Juana, and Emma accompany him on the train to the capital. Naty Revuelta is no more than a face in the crowd.

After his return to Havana, Naty and Fidel do come together again. And finally, after passion has already cooled, at least for Fidel, they make love to each other. They meet in the modest, cramped apartment Fidel's sister Lidia has rented for him. But it is no more than a coda; two months after his release, Fidel has left Havana and Naty.

Strangely silent about that time, Naty never mentions their physical intimacy. I have the sense that she doesn't care about the sexuality between them, that she merely used it to try to hold on to him. But the man she wants, the prisoner who wrote to her, whose hours she filled with her books and letters, that man will never come back.

An ethos, a coming revolution, separates them. She dances; he doesn't. She waits for him; he doesn't even know he's late. Making love to Naty counts little to Fidel; the prospect of General Batista's fleeing, the crowds cheering, the politics of revolution—that's what exhilarates him. (An ominous note: Fidel hands her the letters he's received from her, urging her to keep them with those he's written her from prison, because they will be important for the history of the revolution.)

ANOTHER scene. In her house in the Vedado, more than a year after Fidel's release from prison, Naty sits on the flowered chaise in her sitting room. She loves this quiet time given over to musing about Fidel and about their daughter, Alina, asleep in the nursery. *Esta niña linda que nació de día, quiere que la lleven a la dulcería,* she sings to herself. (This beautiful child, born in the light of day, wishes to be taken to the kingdom of the caramels.)

Naty became pregnant before Fidel left Havana for Mexico City, where he would plan the revolution. "I didn't tell a soul that Fidel and I were having a child. I was certain that it would be a boy, a form of his immortality. I believed that Fidel wouldn't survive the revolution and that the child would be what I had left of him." In this fantasy of a miniature Fidel, Naty has captured the elusive hero she can control forever. It's

Top: Naty's cherished photographs of Fidel and her daughters.
Above: A revolutionary Naty in 1960. Below: The domestic
Naty with her daughters in 1960.

in keeping with her character, a desire to have what she wants—and to have it on her own terms.

When Naty tells me this, I ask her about Orlando, who seems so marginal in her story. Irritated that I wonder whether she thinks herself cruel and insensitive to him, Naty makes me understand that I am testing her patience. She says, "After Fidel became my lover, I began to distance myself from Orlando. I told him that I didn't want to leave him, but that I couldn't share his bed. Once I had a sexual connection to Fidel, I had no alternative but to retreat from my husband."

Still, I ask her: "Who did Orlando believe was the father of your expected child?" If the possibility existed that it was Orlando, I suggest, then she hadn't made such a clean break. Now I've angered her. A reputation as a moral woman, one who hadn't been destructive, that's what matters to her. "Orlando and I didn't talk about it," she says. "Everything went on as it always had. A good man, Orlando took life as it came."

When Fidel learned that Naty was pregnant, he asked her to follow him to Mexico, where he promised to marry her. She refused. How many women with two children would have given up everything to run away with an increasingly unreliable lover? Perhaps the actual man frightened her. Contained excitement, that's what she liked—a lover in prison, his miniature version fast asleep in the nursery. It was certainly preferable to life on the run.

FINAL scene. In her bedroom, Naty now paces as she chain-smokes, scattering ashes on the polished wooden floor, rubbing them into the wood with the toe of her high-heeled shoe. She has not heard from Fidel in a long time, not since the preoccupied letter written soon after his arrival in Mexico: "I'm constantly thinking about Cuba, of my companions, of the obstacles that may lie ahead and of how to overcome them." He went on to ask her to contact comrades, raise funds, send an emissary to let him know what was happening in Havana.

On March 19, 1956, soon after Alina is born, Naty writes to Fidel in Mexico. With the letter, she sends him a little piece of the satin ribbon from his daughter's christening dress. So conventional, even innocent a gesture is a sign that Naty will never break from her bourgeois world, that she can be devoted to Fidel, but not completely to the revolution.

Fidel celebrates with his friends; they raise their glasses and toast the birth of his daughter. Naty celebrates Alina's birth with her mother, Doña Natica, who opens a bottle of champagne to drink to the glorious future. An innocent Doña Natica tells her friends that Alina looks just like Orlando.

It would never have occurred to Herbert Clews' daughter that her infant granddaughter could be moving into dangerous eddies. But it was Doña Natica who used to recite: *"Los hijos de mi madre mis hermanos son, pero los hijos de mi padre son o no son."* ("My mother's children are my brothers and sisters. But as for my father's children, who really knows?")

While in Mexico, Fidel falls in love with a young woman named Isabel Custodio. Naty meanwhile celebrates her thirtieth birthday with her husband and her two daughters. Her intimate time with Fidel is over, but as she writes to him in her last letter: "I seem to say farewell all the time, but I never really go away."

CHAPTER 6

Fidel Castro's Daughter

WHEN Alina Fernández Revuelta was ten years old, she learned that Fidel Castro was her father. The fact of her paternity didn't seem in any way unnatural to her. She remembered the bearded figure who had once been a frequent visitor. He was restless and intense—a virile man whose energy charged her own young spirit. And she looked forward to those early mornings when her mother would awaken her to play with him. Alina and Fidel must have played endless rounds of "hide-and-seek"—a game that rewards intrigue and cunning. Alina never really knew whether she had won or lost; her father, of course, made up his own rules. If she found him hiding behind the plants in the blue-tiled patio, he would laugh and say he wasn't there at all. All in her mind, it must have been a trick of the eye.

Children are drawn to the marvelous; they have no fear of magical transformations. When frogs turn into princes and revolutionary leaders become fathers, children don't always find it astonishing. But Alina absorbed the extraordinary truth about her birth with more than the expected grace, perhaps because her life didn't change at all: the seas did not part, no furious bolts of lightning struck the house. There weren't even extra rations of milk or handouts of forbidden chocolates. For Alina, the world had begun to change long before she learned that Fidel Castro was her father.

I M A G I N E an evening in Havana in 1958. In a stately house in the Vedado—the older, residential part of the city—there is a flurry of activity. Chucha, the cook, is preparing a traditional flan. She watches the brown sugar as it bubbles, just before it caramelizes, creating a minor turmoil in the heavy saucepan. (Chucha sleeps with leaves under her pillow and sprinkles the children's rooms with water to get rid of evil spirits.) Tata, the nursemaid, is complaining about her feet, swollen and aching from running after Alina in Havana's Central Park. Will the black stone she's hidden in Alina's clothes protect the little girl? She worries about Alina more than about her sister, Nina, who seems able to protect herself.

In his medical consulting rooms on the other side of the house, Orlando Fernández tells a patient that there's nothing wrong with his heart. The man seems sullen, as though Orlando had stolen his tragedy from him, deflated him, made him ordinary. It would be hard for Orlando to grasp that some people imagine themselves as heroic, larger than life; he's seen too many people die. There isn't much of a difference in the end, he'd say, between the rich and the poor, the good and the evil. When one of General Batista's military butchers—a dreadful man, shot in the stomach while having dinner at the Sans Souci—was brought into Orlando's operating room, he looked, for all the world, like an angel on the ceiling of the Sistine Chapel.

Inside the nursery, where Nina and Alina have their bedrooms, the walls are rose-colored, the tufted chairs covered in stripes of blue. Tata, bent posture betraying her advancing age, combs two-year-old Alina's hair. Nina, a serious girl of nine, sits quietly in a chair. Resisting Tata's efforts to fasten a blue ribbon in her curls, Alina slithers out of her arms, down the wide stairs, and across to the other side of the house. She is drawn to the X-ray machine, the fluorescent lights, the smell of antiseptic, and, of course, to Orlando. But she can't see him then, not just then.

At the end of the day, Alina's moment of excitement finally arrives. The door to her bedroom opens wide, and Orlando comes striding through. He leans over and stretches out his arms to receive Alina, who runs to him. Then Orlando hugs her until she finally wiggles out of his embrace. Long after the doctor has fled Fidel's island, taking Nina with him, this evening ritual of affection will remain Alina's model for love.

EARLY on New Year's Day in 1959, when Alina was almost three years old, General Batista prepared for exile. Even though Fidel was far from Havana, the dictator was in a hopeless situation: he was losing the support of the army; the rebels had taken over the significant military posts in a number of cities on the island. General Batista managed his leavetaking like a Central Casting tyrant on the run—in a long black Cadillac limousine, his military aides surrounding him, his guests still in evening dress, his guards carrying machine guns. At two in the morning, bound for Miami, he shuttled to the airfield. Right behind him came Meyer Lansky, who chartered a flight to Jacksonville (much to the consternation of that city's district attorney).

When Fidel heard about Batista's flight, he was in Oriente, on the other end of the island, eating a breakfast of chicken with rice and *café con leche*. It was a final private moment.

On January 2, 1959, Fidel Castro entered Santiago. Because it was a symbol, his soldiers assumed command of the Moncada garrison where the revolution began on July 26, 1953. That evening, according to historian Tad Szulc, Fidel set the nationalist, anti-American tone for Cuba's future: "The revolution begins now. . . . This time, luckily for Cuba, the Revolution will truly come into power. It will not be like 1898, when the North Americans came and made themselves masters of our country. . . . The Revolution will not be made in two days, but now I am sure that we are making the Revolution; that for the first time the republic will really be entirely free and the people will have what they deserve. . . ."

Fidel's six-hundred-mile journey from Santiago to Havana bore comparison to the march of a victorious Roman emperor— or so wrote several of his biographers. Cheering crowds greeted him: *Gracias Fidel. Gracias Fidel.* The rebel hero and his entourage—*barbudos* (Castro's guerrillas), recently converted Batistianos, army tanks, jeeps, with Sikorsky helicopters flying overhead—had the aura of gods as their procession moved along the Central Highway for the five days it would take them to reach Havana.

When Fidel entered Havana, dressed in olive-green fatigues—a cigar between his teeth, a medallion of the Virgen del Cobre around his neck—the Cubans greeted him with adoration. A portrait of the charismatic leader, recalls Tad Szulc, showed his heavily bearded face framed with "a Christ-like halo." At Camp Columbia, a white dove (sacred to the Afro-Cuban deities) landed on his shoulder and remained there while he gave his speech. Many Cubans thought it possible that Fidel Castro might, indeed, be Jesus Christ.

ON THE morning of January 8, Naty Revuelta left her house early. The crowds were gathering, and she told her husband that she needed extra time to get through the traffic to her office building. In reality, she had gone out at that hour because she was restless, unsure of herself. Everything seemed to have careened out of control, as Fidel became the anointed leader of the Cuban people.

For so long, Naty's connection to Fidel had been entirely private, the means by which she had lifted herself into a world of bold, refined sentiments. Her passion for Fidel had helped to make her marriage to Orlando last as long as it had. Without Orlando, Naty would have experienced terror, like a stunt woman hurtling through the air, unmoored and unhinged. Yet, without the romance of Fidel, she would have had no patience for Orlando.

Fidel had escaped. He had moved far from his prison cell on the Isle of Pines—and far from her. But Naty couldn't believe that Fidel wouldn't invite her to share his place in the sun. A lover, even when he vanishes from sight, is hard to forget. How much more difficult if he's the national obsession: his face on billboards, his voice dominating the airwaves, his words on everyone's lips.

Outside Naty's house, a woman claiming to be Fidel's childhood friend enchanted a small audience with stories of riding in the hills with the rebel commander when he was a boy, and swimming with him in Oriente's Birán River. In front of the Esso building, Naty ran into friends who herded her towards the procession. The crowds were chanting, *"¡Fidel,*

Naty and her husband,
Orlando, at home

Alina and Tata,
her nursemaid

Fidel, Fidel, viva Fidel!" and raining confetti on the rebel soldiers. ("I have never seen such respect and awe," wrote Ruby Hart Phillips in the *New York Times*.)

Behind a mask of gaiety and high spirits, Naty was able to hide her sadness. Someone thrust a white flower into her hand as Fidel passed in front of her. Naty remembers that she handed the flower to Fidel, who said: *"Mañana te mando a buscar."* ("Tomorrow, I'll send for you.")

When Naty told me about her life after Fidel's rise to power, she was sitting on her terrace, wearing a black dress and the brooch made for her by Wilfredo Lam. Her voice was low, her tone measured. "When he first returned to Havana, I thought that everything would be normal. But it wasn't. For several months we wouldn't see him, and then he'd visit us again. By the end of 1960, he didn't come at all. I wrote him two letters and he never answered them. It was clear that I had to start living my own life without him. I was very depressed. It was very difficult for me. You see, I really loved Fidel."

After Fidel's arrival in Havana, Naty had made a few visits to his headquarters on the twenty-third floor of the Havana Hilton, where he granted audiences—often from his bed, dressed in a pair of striped pajamas. Entering his rooms, she tried to charm him, but Fidel didn't even glance at her. Once, she admired his white typewriter, a portable Olympic, and he urged her to take it home with her. As though she owed him his peace in return for parting with the typewriter, Fidel abruptly ushered her out the door.

ALINA didn't notice when the movers took her bed, the tufted chair, and the carved armoire and carried them away from the comfortable house in the Vedado. But waking up in an undistinguished flat on the other side of the Almendares River, without

Orlando and Nina, must have been traumatic for her. As a young child, Alina couldn't have known that her mother had asked Orlando for a separation. Naty had confessed to her unsuspecting husband that Alina was Fidel's child. Alina would never hear from Orlando or Nina again. Shortly after Naty's confession, and because his medical clinic had been nationalized, Orlando took Nina and went into exile in the United States.

For several months after that, Fidel resumed his visits to Alina. In the middle of the night, he would arrive at the flat as though that were a normal time to call on a five-year-old. He brought clamor and noise, changing the usual languid rhythms of the house to a staccato beat. The lavishness of his energy breathed life into the diminished family. But then, suddenly and without warning, there were no more visits.

Probably, Fidel found it uncomfortable to confront Alina's mother, whom he no longer loved, each time he came to see his daughter. "It is a dreadful misfortune not to be loved when we are in love," the French novelist Benjamin Constant once said, "but it is even more dreadful to be loved passionately when we have ceased to love."

Fidel also frowned on having Alina brought to him at the Presidential Palace or to the *escalinata* of the university, where he had once met with Naty years before. After the end of the regular visits, when Alina was little more than a toddler, Fidel Castro was to limit himself to grand, erratic entrances into Alina's life. He refused to legitimize her by giving her his name. According to Naty, his resistance had to do with Alina's being Orlando's legal child, but it's hard to believe that Fidel would be swayed by another man's rights or the country's laws.

Fidel's desire to dominate a young woman would eventually replace his impulse to visit with a little girl. It wasn't Alina's character that would make Fidel want to bend her to his will, but his own narcissism, his own grandiose imagining of himself—the vanity, the power, the glory, the exalted sense of himself as a redeemer. Alina was a minor player in this pageant of egotism.

Naty doesn't believe that Fidel spends a second thinking about her, or about his only daughter, anymore. But she has her reminders—photographs of Alina in a white party dress with her father, of Fidel laughing, holding a cigar—that there was a moment when he did care. When that moment was over, Naty hit bottom: "I lost thirty-five pounds; there was no work for me, because Esso had closed its offices; the marriage to Orlando had ended, my elder daughter was going to the United States with her father; and Fidel and I had no future together. My mother was devastated. I had lost everything that she valued. And, of course, I still loved Fidel."

WHEN I met Alina in the fall of 1992, she was so pale and thin that she was almost luminous, an angel with bulimia. She barely smiled and had a distant, remote expression in her large brown eyes. There was something unmoving in her face, as though a magician had put a spell on her. She had moved to a run-down flat across the street from her mother's house, a neighborhood where everyone thought of her as her father's daughter. Far away, in the land of fairy tales, the king's beloved daughter inherits the kingdom and lives happily ever after with her prince. But Alina was the ruler's illegitimate child: Fidel never even introduced her to his family; the island kingdom was a wasteland, and the legacy was an ambiguous identity.

Fidel Castro's daughter was a fiction the media had created and occasionally revived. She existed only when the cameras were on her and the lights were flashing. Alina wasn't the character, "Fidel Castro's daughter," at all, but a lonely, frightened young woman in search of a self that ever eluded her.

For years, Alina gave little thought to Fidel. She spent her childhood in her mother's small flat at a time when Havana was starting to become drab and forlorn. Most Cubans will tell you that Havana actually died in March 1968, when Alina turned twelve. That is when Fidel Castro closed the small businesses that lent their color and texture to life in the city: the cafés, the pawnshops, the laundries and hardware stores, the shops where people gathered to tell their stories, and the bars where they had a beer or a Bacardi rum. But Doña Natica had begun to mourn the death of her city much earlier, when Orlando's clinic was nationalized, when her favorite seamstress, Nelly, left for Miami, and when Chucha could no longer find fresh oysters for Sunday dinner.

Would Alina have noticed the small changes when she was a little girl? She wouldn't have known that La Época and El Encanto, the leading department stores, were sabotaged and burned to the ground. Her mother wouldn't have mentioned the government's seizure of the Havana Hilton, the Hotel Nacional, the Capri, and the Riviera. She wouldn't have missed dancing the night away at the Sans Souci. Probably no one even thought to tell Alina that the Beatles were banned. But she might have gazed at the billboard with the revolutionary Nativity scene in which Fidel Castro, Che Guevara, and Major Almeida, the chief of the army, played the three wise men. Among the gifts they brought were Agrarian Reform, Urban Reform, and the Year of Education.

As long as the boundaries of Alina's world remained home and school, that's where she experienced anger, separation, futility. Orlando's departure must have been awful for her, although by the time I first met Alina he had become a faint memory. With no warning, her friends sometimes fled across the straits, joining her lost father and sister in the United States. And Cuban children were encouraged not to write to those in exile—they were *gusanos* who had chosen to betray the revolution. After Lisette Santamaría, Alina's dearest friend (she had had dinner with the Santamarías whenever she could), flew away, Alina never heard from her again. Naty didn't even write to her daughter Nina, because Fidel demanded that loyalists sever personal ties—even with their children, if they had turned their backs on Cuba.

At home, there was never anything to eat except *frijoles* and rice, albeit served by a maid on a silver platter. Such scarcity was unusual in a household as well connected as the one in which Alina lived. In those years, Fidel provided those around him with many luxuries. It was even rumored that he made it possible for the elephant at the Havana Zoo to eat an omelet made of ninety-nine eggs. (It would have been a hundred, but the cook stole one a day for his wife.) Alina's mother, however, refused to tap into either Fidel's largesse or the black market, hoping he would learn that she had sacrificed herself, and even his own daughter, for the revolution.

If the food was monotonous, the dinner hour was not. Alina and her mother had to endure outbursts of rage from Doña Natica. *"¡Mira! No sabes ni comer bien."* ("Look! You don't even know how to eat.") She never missed the opportunity to insult Naty for having separated from Orlando and abandoned her daughter Nina, whom Doña Natica elevated to household saint. Shards of this rage pressed in on every conversation— her anger that her daughter had banished the original, true family, and that without them Doña Natica was bereft.

Towards Alina, Doña Natica was cold and unfriendly. Alina described to me how her grandmother would arrive with a long needle—the little girl could see that it made the older woman feel powerful —and give Alina injections of vitamins. When Chucha left and Doña Natica began to cook for the family, Alina would sit at the dining-room table refusing to touch the food. Her grandmother demanded praise; her mother fought with her over the value of nourishment. As Alina grew older, her connection to food would become more furtive. Alone in her room, she would eat and purge, which led to the emaciation typical of bulimia.

After Fidel withdrew from her life, Naty was devastated. Severely depressed and working hard for the government, she hadn't much energy to put into her daughters. Speaking of this period in her life, some members of Naty's circle criticize her for allowing Nina to leave home. In their eyes, Naty's every move has been calculated to win back Fidel; they even speculate that Naty let Nina go so that Fidel would be drawn to a household where the one remaining child was his own.

Later, Naty told her own version of the story. "When Orlando was about to leave, Nina asked me for permission to go with him for a year. She said: 'You have everything and my father has nothing. . . . He doesn't know the language in the United States. He has to study, to revalidate his medical license, and I want to be with him. I can go to school there, but I'll be home in less than a year.' I agreed.

"Orlando promised that I'd have Nina back in nine months, but he never sent her home. What could I do? Who was going to listen to me? What court in the United States would have heard me if I had said that I wanted Nina returned to me?" Naty continues: "Nina was so like her father, it made sense for her to want to be with him. In 1964, when I went to Paris with Alina, I asked Orlando to send Nina to me for a visit, but he refused. I didn't struggle. I never press people. In the end, I didn't see Nina for more than twenty years."

As for Alina, Naty spent hardly a minute with her. Mothering was demanded of Naty during a time when she couldn't concentrate on it. Even Fidel, at scattered moments, showed more concern about Alina's care. The child had lived on a diet of lentils boiled without salt for more than a week preceding a rare visit from her father. Fidel found her undernourished and ordered special milk for her. Naty, self-absorbed, drawn into herself, had no time for her daughter. "I was working so hard for the revolution," she told me. "I used to get home when Alina was fast asleep. In the morning, I would give her a rushed kiss and I'd be off to work again."

Even Naty had to notice that her daughter was withdrawing into an imaginary world. "When I saw how much she needed me, how she cried when I left, I began to wonder if there wasn't something of a weakness in her soul." Sometimes Alina drew little girls sitting on the moon or dancing on top of the sun. More often, she sketched beautiful women who had their backs turned to her. Alina never drew the figure of a man.

In 1964, Fidel posted Naty to the Cuban Embassy in Paris. He was eager to be rid of his tiresome former mistress and an eight-year-old daughter. He even offered to send Naty's mother along—and Tata, the nursemaid. Sometimes I see Fidel as the master chess player, and Naty as a rather clumsy opponent, castling the bishop, sacrificing her pawns, being outmaneuvered, but staying in the game. Perhaps Fidel thought that they wouldn't come back from Paris, but Naty would never have accepted a permanent exile.

Soon after their arrival in Paris, Naty decided to place her daughter in a school at Saint-Germain-en-Laye, about ten miles outside the city. Taken to the *pension* where she would board while attending classes, Alina was terrified. She hid behind her mother's dress, pulling on the belt, until Naty wrenched herself free. With every French phrase she heard, the child panicked. Her only defense was to hang on to her mother, then to push and kick the woman assigned to take care of her. Small, thin Alina was no match for Naty and the French administrator.

Years later she recalled, "We'd been in Paris for just three days when my mother sent me away. I was terrified. I couldn't even say *oui*. I didn't know how to tie my own shoes. I didn't even know French existed." Alina, who claims that she was constantly vomiting from a diet of rhubarb and artichokes, boarded in the country all week; on Saturday afternoon, her mother retrieved her and brought her home for the night, then returned her to the *pension* on Sunday evening. To make things worse, Naty often worked through their Saturday nights together, completing a study of the French chemical industry that Fidel had asked her to do in her spare time.

Even though the missile crisis was over, Naty feared a possible American invasion of Cuba. Yet, at the end of Doña Natica's visit to Paris, Naty sent Alina home with her grandmother. What prompted her to send her daughter back to Havana at a moment she perceived as potentially dangerous? Wasn't it done out of devotion to Fidel?

IN HAVANA, when Alina told me about her childhood, there was no humor or lightness to the tale; the bitterness still prevailed. Her private feelings weren't valued. How else to explain her humiliation when she wrote a love poem to her mother and learned that Naty had had it published in the Communist youth magazine? Alina increasingly turned in on herself, separating from everyone else. Even when her beloved Tata became ill, Alina refused to visit her. Instead, she felt herself turning to stone. The death of feeling was the legacy of her early childhood.

Not long after Naty returned to Havana, in 1966, she

decided that it was time to tell Alina about her real father. Alina was ten years old and struggling with her first crocodile. Naty had received the beast as a gift from her new colleagues at Havana's CNIC, the Center for Scientific Research. The crocodile lived in the bathtub, where Alina could care for it. What took precedence for her was the drama of the crocodile, not the announcement about Fidel.

The actual moment of Naty's revelation was flat and undramatic, or that's how both women remember it. Naty: "We were taking a walk in a little park in front of our house when I told her. It was intuitive. It was logical, really. For a long time, I had prepared her. I used to tell her that her hands and her feet were like Fidel's. When she made a fist, I said that she reminded me of him. I wanted to tell her that he was her father before someone else did. After all, there were many people who knew, and some who wanted to be cruel. When I finally revealed the secret, she was gracious about it. More to the point, she seemed very happy."

Alina's version is just as matter-of-fact. "I guess I prompted the conversation. . . . It certainly wasn't terrible to learn that I was Fidel's daughter. He was, after all, Fidel Castro. And at that time, everyone was for him. I remember that, at the movies, when he appeared on the screen, everyone applauded. . . . And I wasn't very surprised, not really. Probably, I had a preconceived notion that he might be my father. After all, he came to visit me—not consistently, perhaps, but he did come. Once he brought me a doll, a figure of a rebel soldier with a beard. It didn't matter that he came sporadically, and that when I was small he would come in the middle of the night. Since Orlando had gone from the island, those rare visits of Fidel's were all I knew of being fathered."

To many of Naty's remaining friends in Havana, she was the villain in this particular story. Most thought that revealing

Alina's parentage to her was selfish and manipulative. It's hard
not to be judgmental, to ignore a mother's moral insensitivity.
Certainly, Naty compromised Alina's sense of herself. But for
Naty, the connection to Fidel had become the justification for
her existence. She needed to differentiate herself from the others who adored him. That was how she did it, by making it
known that her daughter Alina was his child.

Sentencing Alina to illegitimacy (no small thing in a Latin
American culture) condemned her to a second abandonment.
She would never be given Fidel's name. Only rarely included
in the Castro family festivities—and then only by Raúl Castro
and his wife—she wouldn't even be introduced to Fidel's sons,
her half-brothers. (Fidel Castro's personal life is rarely mentioned in public in Havana. It is rumored that he lives with
Delia Soto del Valle, with whom he has six sons.) "I was born,"
Alina has often said, "just to improve my mother's position
with Fidel. And because of me, she has received privileges that
might not otherwise have been hers. That's all."

Soon after Alina learned that she was Fidel's daughter, he
vanished from her life. He sent for his daughter twice, no more
than that, in the next several years. Once, late at night, he sent
an aide in an Alfa Romeo to fetch her so that she could watch
him play basketball. Whenever Fidel made a basket, both teams
shouted *"¡Viva Fidel!"* Another time, he asked if she wanted
to go to a movie. She longed to see *The Godfather;* her father
treated her instead to a screening of a film about his triumphal
tour of Eastern Europe.

In her early adolescence, Alina had meager psychological
resources of her own, needed more of them to reinvent herself,
and had no kind guide to help her. Her bouts of anorexia and
bulimia, her refusal to eat at the dining-room table with anyone
else present, reflected her rebellion against a dominating
mother and grandmother. Alina was confused, frightened, and

undernourished. Her eating disorder would remain with her, making it possible for her to hide from pain in the body of a child.

IN 1972, at the age of sixteen, Alina became engaged to a military officer twice her age who worked for the Ministry of the Interior. (Doña Natica was not pleased that Alina's fiancé's most recent wife was a black woman.) Naty called Fidel, whom she hadn't seen in a very long time, to ask that he arrange for a wedding cake. Although the government promised to provide each bride with a cake, a pair of white shoes, and a case of refreshments, the head of state was usually not involved. In response, Fidel sent an ill-humored driver in an Alfa Romeo to fetch his daughter to the Presidential Palace. When Alina arrived at two in the morning, security guards escorted her into an elevator, and she descended to the small subterranean office where her angry father awaited her.

Like a patriarch in a nineteenth-century novel, Fidel railed at Alina for having chosen to marry a divorced man he thought an opportunist, and for not having sought his permission before she announced her engagement. A man who demanded total control, her father would not be satisfied with the marginal role of purveyor of his daughter's wedding cake. Only when Alina agreed to delay the wedding, and to hold the ceremony whenever Fidel wished, did he agree not only to attend but to furnish the wedding feast. Things went well between them, for the last time. She had posed a challenge, and he had risen to it—the game he relished most.

The wedding was held in the Nuevo Vedado, in the stone house to which Doña Natica, Naty, and Alina had moved in 1970. A hundred guests came to see the bride in her long white dress—a fine-boned girl, haunting in her thinness, with the look of a frightened gazelle. The groom seemed nervous—his stature reduced to almost nothing when Fidel entered the room—and embarrassed at having to present himself to his leader in this setting.

With little to eat or drink, it didn't prove to be much of a grand occasion. (Fidel brought four bottles of rum to go around, a liter of scotch for himself, and a large pasta salad decorated with pineapple.) But the assembled guests were so thrilled to be with Fidel—men and women alike fawned on him—that no one but Doña Natica complained about the meager bridal buffet. She added miserliness to her ever-growing list of Fidel's sins.

THE PRODUCT of an angry world, Alina was troublesome and volatile. In an allegory about Cuba, her father would represent Power; Alina, Damage—the fruit of the revolution. When I first interviewed her in Havana, she frightened me. Even then, when it seemed that we were getting on, I suspected that our relationship wouldn't last. Many people had difficulty staying connected to Alina. That's the way she was. I couldn't expect anything else.

None of Alina's marriages lasted more than a year. "In terms of marriage," Alina often said, "I'm an annual, not a perennial." But the truth was more complicated than that. In her hasty descriptions, her husbands never seemed real—more like cartoon sketches of men. Talking about them, she never used their proper names, reducing them to stick-figure abstractions: *el militar, el héroe, el bailarín, el millonario.* (In Havana, when we attended an aerobics class together, she never even mentioned that our instructor was her first husband.)

Alina's second husband, a soldier stationed in Angola, had resented his permanent place on the dangerous front lines.

Fidel had ordered that there be no special treatment for his son-in-law. He divorced her, according to Alina, to get out from under Fidel's thumb. After that, Alina married a dancer, the father of her daughter, Mumín, who was born in 1977, the year Alina turned twenty-one. (Fidel had said: *"¿Cómo es posible que hayas dejado un héroe de Angola por un bailarín?"* ["How could you have left a war hero for a ballet dancer?"]) After their inevitable separation, Alina resented Panchi the most because her mother invited him to live in her house, insisting that Mumín needed the presence of her father. To Alina, her mother's gesture was another serious betrayal.

Soon after that divorce, Alina married a well-to-do investor from Mexico. Convinced that her daughter's marriage to a foreigner would infuriate Fidel, surely Naty overestimated its impact when she said it would be like a bomb falling on Havana. Still, when Alina's husband wanted to take her out of the country, Fidel did deny his daughter a permit to travel. This occasioned a bitter dialogue between Alina and her father, filled with anger and recriminations. "It was humiliating," said Alina. "After that, I became very aggressive. My husband began to distance himself from me." The marriage, continuing her pattern, was over in a year.

We talked about it. "If you love someone, you don't just abandon him because he's flawed," I said. But Alina seemed able to do just that. I came away with the sense that Alina takes flight at the first sign of disagreement; that she can't remember when someone has been good to her, and so, if a man's empathy fails even once, she banishes him from her affections. I wondered if, for Alina, the present doesn't erase the past—so that the last thing that happens to her negates everything else.

In the seasons of her marriages, Alina had perfected her role as the rebel daughter. Now she was blaming Fidel, not just

Mumín Salgado

Mumín
before her ballet
recital, 1983

for the marriages, but for her failure to find meaningful work. She had gone to medical school for a while, studied international relations, trained at the Teatro Nacional, and worked for the Ministry of Culture. Modeling at La Maison, a popular restaurant with an evening fashion show, was the closest Alina came to having work she relished, even though she didn't get along with the other mannequins. "I'm an anarchist," she often said, "I'm not responsible."

But from that fragile place where one's sense of self emerges came Alina's anguish, her confusion, her sense of entitlement. Wouldn't it have been better had she not known that Fidel was her father? Had she never been told, had she learned to use her considerable intelligence, she could have lived by her wits. There would have been talk, rumors about her dubious parentage, but everything would have died down. Had Orlando not known, he would have taken her with him. She could have emigrated, enjoying his paternal affection and protection. A father is a father when he acts like one.

Without Prospero's magic tricks to transform her island existence, Alina had to rely on the shiniest baubles for comfort. She fell in love with designer clothes, and with diamonds and pearls—her substitutes for love.

Perhaps the blessed are those who can travel to islands but aren't confined to them. Surrounded by water, isolated from the rest of the world, an island assumes the contours of the inhabitants' own imaginings. In Cuba, since the emergence of Fidel Castro, the people have allowed a single man to determine the emotional geography of the entire island. A grand sorcerer, Fidel enchanted the Cubans, making them believe that both he and the island were almighty, and invincible.

To be sure, Fidel has aimed missiles at the United States, sent his soldiers to Angola, pretended not to care when the Soviet Union no longer existed to give massive infusions to the island economy. And he has, of course, manipulated his larger-than-life image. The mythological hero is never photographed doing the ordinary—eating, drinking, playing with the children—but, rather, striding, strutting, a Homeric figure in familiar green fatigues.

Today, when there is no longer a romantic revolution (it survives only in Fidel's mind and in the memories of his aging supporters), many islanders, frustrated with the failure of their ideals, have turned to the United States, the government's scapegoat, for hope. Naty's generation, which gave everything to Fidel, can't negotiate the acrobatic reversal with ease. People of Alina's age, however, who know the revolution through confinement, scarcity, and despair, dream of flight to the United States. Since so little knowledge of the States filters through the censored press, these children, like immigrants before them, imagine that across the blue waters lies a proverbial Eden.

Even if that paradise was a dream of Alina's, after four failed marriages and her estrangement from Fidel, she felt defeated, enervated. In a severe depression, she crawled into bed, swallowing medications that placed her in a state of limbo. For months at a time, she was treated at a special hospital, only available to her because she was Fidel's daughter.

I I

THERE were enough similarities in their backgrounds to make Alina Fernández and Osvaldo Rodríguez feel like twins. Both had strong, hard, beautiful mothers and absent, legendary fathers. Their parents were people who had asked of life that it be intense, free of such conventional obligations as the creation of a home and the rearing of children. Osvaldo's mother, Marta Jiménez, was a brilliant, successful diplomat, serving Castro's Cuba as an ambassador to the United Nations, to Denmark, and to Switzerland. She was competent and formal, presenting herself with a certain revolutionary *gravitas* that Fidel admired in women. Her late husband, Fructuoso Rodríguez, Osvaldo's father, had been a leader of the student movement against Batista. He gave his life for the cause at the beginning of the revolution. That early death assured him of an immortality that even Fidel might find enviable.

When Osvaldo was born, months after his father's death, courtiers in green fatigues gathered round the cradle to celebrate the birth. Something of being the *jeunesse dorée* of the revolution would cling to both Alina and Osvaldo, but with differences. Osvaldo was the legitimate child of a hero; Alina, the invisible child of that hero's leader.

As teenagers, Alina and Osvaldo became more than just friends; their connection was fraternal, almost conspiratorial. They shared secret dreams, driven by impulses that were somewhat anarchic. Both had preoccupied parents, a fundamental restlessness, a conviction that they could trust each other. They believed that together they could transcend the limitations of their island life. The courts of kings and those of Communist leaders thrive on hierarchies, and position determines privilege. Herein is the decline, the rot, of revolution: a dream of social justice fades, replaced not by idealism but with favoritism. The chosen circle the leader like ravenous vultures.

Alina and Osvaldo, who missed the romance of the Sierra Maestra, lived in the realities created by Fidel's abuse of power. Osvaldo was heir to the inner circle of political influence. That anchoring alone secured him a place at court. He taught himself to understand patronage, to savor the delicacies offered to the favored, to accept the privileges that attend a fortunate birth. In the Presidential Palace, at celebrations hosted by the government, he sat with other guests at linen-covered tables adorned with roses, eating Cuban lobster and Russian caviar

Alina in Havana, 1989

and drinking champagne. Courtier Osvaldo met Leonid Brezhnev, Andrei Gromyko, and Yasser Arafat.

Unlike Osvaldo, Alina never became a part of Fidel's world. When her cousin Deborah (Raúl Castro's daughter) married, Alina was not invited. Osvaldo, who was, brought her as his date. When Alina entered the room, wearing a provocative claret dress, the neckline plunging, uncomfortable guests removed themselves from her side. At Osvaldo's instigation, the photographers moved closer.

Osvaldo, loyal only to Alina, never missed a chance to make the *comandante* uncomfortable. "Fidel, I want to have my photograph taken with you." The dictator smiled. A group formed around Fidel: Raúl and his wife, Vilma; Osvaldo; Deborah. Everyone smiled. At the last minute, Osvaldo grabbed Alina's hand, drawing her into the portrait. Smiles still all around. The photograph, framed in silver, was a travesty of an affectionate father and daughter attending a family wedding.

The revolution had grown complacent, self-centered. In the most conventional matters, privilege asserted itself. The Ministry of the Interior had "lists" of those eligible for food delicacies, for furniture, for flights around the world. There was even *la lista de la orquídea* that entitled those of Osvaldo's status to order special flowers. Most people had to honor their dead with a single blossom or two, held together with a white paper bow; for a special funeral, however, Osvaldo received a large wreath of flowers tied with a violet bow. Before he went to the Colón cemetery, he removed the satin ribbon and gave it to the delighted little daughter of a friend.

Often, Osvaldo lavished presents on Alina: chocolates, cheese, a lobster. When she needed gasoline, he could fill her car without having to wait in line. Although Alina's name was not on the "lists," she was occasionally given food and some money by the ministry. The party's favors were not automatic, though, and of course she couldn't leave Cuba. Possibly, her ultimate plan to escape had begun to hatch when she was forbidden to travel out of the country with her Mexican husband.

A L I N A and Osvaldo often jogged miles together through the woods, Alina listening to her friend reveal what he had learned about the world *más allá. Allá. Allá todo es mejor.* (Over there. Over there, everything is better.) No Marco Polo, but a privileged heir of the Cuban Revolution, Osvaldo had traveled to Communist countries—the Soviet Union, Poland, and Bulgaria—and, later, to England, France, and Switzerland.

On returning from a trip to the Soviet Union, Osvaldo offered nothing but praise for what Lenin had accomplished. With no anxious thoughts that he might be doubted, he extravagantly praised all the Soviet-bloc nations. What a splendid Communist traveler! No one would have denied him permission to travel to Paris, for example, since he was such an obvious "true believer." He could be counted upon, the powers that be must have believed, to convince the gullible that Paris was to be loathed for its decadence, that it couldn't hold a candle to Cracow, Moscow, or Tirana. The official propaganda he mouthed masked Osvaldo's real travel goals: haunting streets, sitting in cafés, listening to conversations in foreign languages.

Osvaldo's earliest knowledge of the Western world had come from the periodicals that his mother and her friends brought home from their diplomatic travels. He remembers that, accustomed to the coarse, grainy paper of *Bohemia,* the Cuban magazine, he fell in love with the smooth, satiny magazines: *Time, Newsweek, Vogue,* and *Elle.* This was the presentation of the world outside that Alina received from Osvaldo: Palm Beach, BMWs, Armani, Versace, and the Côte d'Azur.

He loved green because it was the color of the American dollar: *"El dólar me mareaba."* ("The dollar made me dizzy.")

Had Cuba's fortunes not changed, Osvaldo would have found all the delights of Western consumerism right at home. Without Fidel's revolution, Cuba would have remained the old familiar place in modern garb. Osvaldo could never imagine this in Cuba, but I can. It was de Soto's dream, Lord Albemarle's, Meyer Lansky's—and even Doña Natica's, with her champagne flutes of French crystal.

Later on, when he had immigrated to the United States, Osvaldo would use consumer language as a code to communicate with Alina. "The red Chanel dress you need is almost ready," he would tell her, when he called Havana from Miami. Alina would know that her fake Spanish passport was about to arrive. But in the time before, when both their lives were still uneventful, the *más allá* was just the dream that kept them running together in the forest of Havana.

Marriage to a foreigner would do the trick for Osvaldo Rodríguez. Wanting to leave Cuba without harming his mother's diplomatic career, he found a graceful exit through the front door. In 1988, an Argentine art dealer who owed Osvaldo a favor offered to lend him his own bride-to-be. This agreeable young woman from Buenos Aires married Osvaldo a few hours after they met in Havana.

A month later, Osvaldo attended a New Year's Day party at the Presidential Palace, confronted Fidel on the receiving line, and secured his personal permission to emigrate. Unfortunately, he argued, his wife couldn't adapt to the customs of a Communist country. Gallantly, probably with a sense of relief, Fidel agreed to let him go. That was only half the battle. Osvaldo was a romantic at heart. He believed that, as long as Alina remained on the island, he himself was not entirely free.

ESCAPE was and is the prevailing theme in Cuban life. *"Balseros,"* braving themselves for the huge waves, flee the island on small rafts, wash up on tiny cays, and drift towards Florida. But it is the larger-than-life image of Orestes Lorenzo that hovers at the edge of everyone's mind. A Cuban fighter pilot—an officer who defected to the United States in a government plane—Orestes Lorenzo borrowed a Cessna in Key West, recrossed the Straits of Florida, managed to land the plane on a public road near Varadero. There he rescued his waiting wife and children and then successfully returned to the Keys. (It's hard to decide whether the cheers for Orestes were louder in Havana or in Miami, where he now lives.)

It was a common commercial airliner that was to transport Alina to freedom. Osvaldo thought about the escape as carefully as had Orestes Lorenzo in planning his daredevil flights. But Osvaldo had to depend upon Alina's peculiar strengths: her sense of play, passion for acting, and penchant for disguises.

As a child, Alina loved to wear costumes and to paint her face. It was a great pleasure to startle her grandmother with a frightening impersonation: a wolf, a skeleton, a gremlin, a witch. When she grew up, Alina continued to play an elaborate game of "Now you see me, now you don't." On the fine planes of her face, she rouged and glossed her skin to change expression, alter contour. She cut her long, dark hair and bleached it the color of carrots. She lined and painted her mouth. Without her makeup, she looked like a startled child: large brown eyes staring out from a narrow, chiseled face. She would stretch her talent for camouflage and self-transformation. If Fidel Castro's daughter could not leave the island, Alina would have to become someone else.

In 1991, as soon as he arrived in Miami, after divorcing his wife in Buenos Aires, Osvaldo Rodríguez started working on his plan to spirit Alina out of Cuba. As the son of a hero of the revolution, it hadn't been easy for him to leave, and it would be doubly hard for Alina. But Osvaldo counted on his own resolve and courage. Together with a stroke of good fortune, they had seen him through his own prolonged ordeal in Cuba.

WHEN Osvaldo presented Armando Valladares, a Cuban-American human-rights activist in Miami, with his plan for Alina's escape, Valladares wasted no time. After his role in Orestes Lorenzo's rescue flight, Armando Valladares was searching for another bold venture with which to humiliate Fidel Castro. He chose a couple of familiar partners. Mari-Paz Martínez-Nieto, Valladares's former assistant in Madrid, called *Paris-Match* and convinced them to finance Alina's flight to freedom in return for exclusive rights to the photographs. Valladares also turned to Elena Amos, godmother of the conservative Cuban-American cause.

For Elena Amos, it was a crusade—a religious war against Satan's forces. A frail, birdlike woman of about seventy, Elena wore a pendant around her neck, a glass orb holding Cuban sand from the beach at Varadero. Her political sentiments, grounded in hatred for Fidel, she owed to her father. In the 1950s, Salvador Díaz-Verson had founded Cuba's anti-Communist league. Even before the future leader came down from the Sierra Maestra, Díaz-Verson had declared in his newspaper column that Fidel Castro was a Marxist.

Around fifty years ago, while a student in Miami, Elena Díaz-Verson was introduced to John Amos. Soon after, they married. In 1990, the elderly Amos died of cancer, leaving his widow a large fortune. With her enormous resources and her conservative political connections, she was eager to go to the barricades. A journalist's daughter, Elena was also clever enough to see the propaganda value of the defection of Fidel's daughter.

With Fernando Espineira, a Spanish friend, Osvaldo engaged the cast of the drama and decided on the time of the performance. He called Alina using a code to tell her that the plan was in motion: *"Te va a ver una persona que te va a dar el vestido rojo de Chanel."* ("Someone who will give you a red dress from Chanel is coming to see you.") And Alina answered: *"¡Qué bien! Me hace mucha falta."* ("Wonderful! I need it very much.")

Osvaldo had returned to Havana several times to see his mother. After his last visit, as he was about to board the plane for Miami, he had noticed the carelessness of the immigration staff. He handed his passport to a bureaucrat who didn't even glance at him when he stamped the document. Alina could have gone right through in his stead, without being noticed. But what if security tightened? By the time his flight landed in Miami, Osvaldo thought he had solved the problem of her escape.

IN MADRID, Mari-Carmen López and Victoria Janeiro, friends of Fernando and Osvaldo's, agreed to board an Iberia flight from Madrid to Havana, posing as Spanish tourists oblivious to politics, eager for the sun. Their love of adventure, their affection for Osvaldo and Fernando, and the sheer lark of traveling to Havana motivated them to take part in the rescue mission. Mari-Carmen was a fierce, energetic woman in her fifties; Victoria, adventurous and more than a decade younger.

When the women arrived at the Hotel Capri, Victoria settled in for a fortnight of reading in the sun. Mari-Carmen never unpacked her bathing suit but went immediately to see Alina at her Nuevo Vedado flat. She brought with her a suitcase of clothes bearing labels from Madrid, and a dreadful brown wig with bangs. Intentionally, Alina had gained weight to add to her disguise, and, wearing the unfortunate synthetic hair, she looked like a frumpy housewife from the south of Spain. Mari-Carmen took an entire roll of photographs of the bewigged, unsmiling Alina.

On the following morning, Mari-Carmen boarded a flight to Mexico City, with the roll of film and Victoria's passport hidden in her suitcase. (Immigration had stamped the document to show that Victoria had entered Cuba legally as a Spanish tourist.) In Mexico, Mari-Carmen gave the passport and the photographs to Fernando, who carried them to his native Madrid. Mari-Carmen then returned to Havana.

In Madrid, a Cuban expert at passport forgery substituted Alina's photograph for Victoria's. A third friend, a Spanish architect with time on his hands, then boarded the Iberia flight to Havana. When he landed, he gave the passport to Mari-Carmen, who gave it to Alina, together with Victoria's return ticket to Spain. Victoria continued to improve her suntan on the terrace of the Hotel Capri, avoiding the journalist from *Paris-Match*, who was eager for the scoop that Alina was leaving.

ON THE morning of December 19, 1993, Alina Fernández Revuelta swore her daughter to secrecy and kissed her goodbye on the cheek. Wearing a gold cap to steady the curly brown wig, she called for a taxi and told the driver to take her to José Martí Airport. The thrill of the danger and the duplicity bolstered her confidence. She stared at the man from Immigration as she handed him her passport, lingered while he chatted with someone, stared at him again as he stamped it and indifferently waved her on. Was it that simple? After being told that she would never leave the island, after having imagined herself on a rubber raft paddling towards Miami, she had walked through her father's barriers in high heels and synthetic curls.

An hour later, on the flight to Madrid, the journalist from *Paris-Match* was the single person who knew who she was. After landing at Barajas Airport, she sailed through immigration and customs with Victoria's passport. Fernando, Osvaldo's partner, and Armando Valladares, the escape's sponsor, embraced her. (Osvaldo had remained in Miami, since he didn't have State Department permission to leave the United States.) With Valladares stood three *Paris-Match* journalists. No one was to mention Alina's arrival, or write about her at all, until *Paris-Match* announced her defection in its December 30 issue.

Victoria, meanwhile, was en route to the Spanish Embassy in Havana, where she pretended that her passport had been stolen and she had missed the flight to Madrid. Granted a document permitting her to leave Cuba, she returned to Spain with Mari-Carmen on the 22nd. Changó, Christ, or Good Fortune beamed on Victoria, who left Havana just hours before *ABC*, a conservative journal in Madrid, leaked the information from Valladares's former assistant that Alina had fled the island on a Spanish passport. In that moment, Alina became fully realized as "Fidel Castro's daughter": a commodity, a celebrity, an abstraction.

At the Hotel Michelangelo in Madrid, Elena Amos waited for Alina. Orestes Lorenzo entered her rooms first—then Alina, whom she greeted with an embrace and the present of a hundred dollars and a green sweater. Elena's first gesture was maternal. She arranged for Alina to return home with her, then called Senator Sam Nunn of Georgia. He intervened with

Immigration, and Fidel's daughter was allowed to enter the United States. After a flight from Madrid to Atlanta, Alina boarded Elena's private plane, which would carry her into the American heartland. She landed, an hour later, in Elena's home town, Columbus, Georgia. (How appropriate for Alina to have entered her new world in a town called Columbus.)

I THOUGHT that I should see Alina again. When she asked me to come, I flew to Atlanta and then Columbus, getting there three days after Christmas. How unreal it had been to see her arrival on television. Surrounded by Elena and Osvaldo, Alina, in a white suit and a strand of soft pearls, had faced the cameras. (Nobody could tell, she told me later, that the pearls were Doña Natica's rosary beads.) And still it went on—this attention to an instant celebrity. Journalists fought for interviews with her; publishers brandished lucrative contracts. Alina, who hadn't so much as heard of Columbus before leaving Cuba, now found herself its most notorious resident.

Situated on the banks of the Chattahoochee River, Columbus, Georgia, is the birthplace of Dr. John S. Pemberton, the inventor of Coca-Cola. In 1876, Edwin Booth performed at the town's Springer Opera House. He and his brother John Wilkes were guests at Esquiline, the Moses family plantation. When Oscar Wilde lectured there, the women of Columbus tossed sunflowers in his path to protect the leather on his fine boots from the mud. Currently, the jeweler in town is none other than My Lai's infamous Lieutenant William Calley.

The AFLAC (American Family Life Assurance Corporation) building, a high-rise monument to John Amos's success in selling cancer insurance, dominates the town. Before he died,

Amos built a triplex penthouse for his beloved Elena— a marble fortress set above the parking garage that overlooks the AFLAC superstructure. Downstairs, at the entrance to this very American Taj Mahal, stand a battery of sentries with cellular phones, poised to defend Elena against suspicious intruders.

I couldn't have set the stage. Goldfinches—mutating finches, I'm told—living in enormous glass cases lined the penthouse's marble entrance halls. The male finches sported brilliant plumage. The duller females spent much of their time preparing crude, cup-shaped nests for their small speckled eggs. In their decorative cages, these songbirds of sultans caroled their sweet song.

Perhaps the finches were the penthouses's royal harbingers —for Elena's house was a princely fantasy. Three stories high, it centered on a large swimming pool, a clear blue pool that might have come from a painting by David Hockney. The grand-house architecture with its elaborate interior design— the wide halls faced in white marble, the faux–Louis XV tables, the formal chairs covered in delicate pastel brocades—heightened the sense of Elena as an imposing patron.

Over this castle-fortress presided Elena's friend, her Cuban-American decorator—a large, heavyset man whose hands were covered in diamond rings. Around his throat, he wore a set of gold chains and a large medal of Santa Bárbara. The white-clad collection of manicurists, maids, and hairdressers who take care of Elena treated him with deference, as though he were the Cardinal Richelieu. In Alina's room, a collection of porcelain dolls with startled faces looked out on the domestic scene in a permanent state of astonishment.

. . .

A NUMBNESS had overtaken her. That evening, Alina told me about the strange detachment she had experienced as she was leaving Havana. "If I don't go," she had thought to herself, "I will grow old here." Nothing more. She hadn't even had an anxious thought about the risks she was taking. Although she described it to me as a rare emotional moment, it didn't seem so to me. In Havana, I had observed in her a lack of affect, the failure of feeling.

Now a celebrity, Alina had to account for her sins. Television had become a huge confessional presided over by a curious order of high priests. Talk-show host Larry King asked Alina if she loved her father. "I do not refer to Mr. Castro as my father," she said. "I do not have a message for him." Why, he continued, had she left her sixteen-year-old daughter behind? Because she didn't know what to do, Alina answered. "The only way I could help Mumín was by coming out first. It was my daughter who pushed me, encouraged me to leave. 'If you don't do it,' Mumín told me, 'I'll never forgive you.'"

Suddenly it became a crusade. To the press, Alina insisted that her only concern was getting her daughter out of Cuba; nothing else mattered. As soon as she pleaded with Fidel to release Mumín, everyone forgave her. Even Jesse Jackson, who had just returned from Havana, offered to intercede with his friend Fidel. But there was no need for that. With his instinct for public relations, Fidel agreed that Mumín could leave the country immediately. Why would he have tried to keep her there? She would retain, he added, her rights and privileges as a citizen of Cuba.

Twelve days after her mother's more dramatic departure, Mumín flew from Havana to Miami. A few hours later, she went to Atlanta, where she was reunited with her mother. Together, they boarded Elena's plane for the short flight to Columbus.

NEW YEAR'S EVE. At midnight, Elena Amos raises her champagne glass and toasts Mumín's safe arrival. Shy, with pale skin and large brown eyes, Mumín resembles a betrothed Spanish *infanta* arriving in a foreign country. Elena, her slim arms covered in golden bracelets, embraces both Alina and her daughter. In her soft voice, Mumín faces the hastily assembled television cameras. She asks for forgiveness from the families of children who haven't been able to get out of Cuba.

After the toasts, Alina and Mumín return to their rooms. Wondering about her dog, Rudi, Mumín imagines what he would be like in her new bedroom, tearing away at the furniture. She tells me that she hopes Grandmother Naty will give him enough attention. It's not something she can discuss with her mother. Alina has no interest in Rudi, never did. Pointing to two small holes in Mumín's dress, she announces that the dress must be thrown away. Mumín, who had worn the dress at her sixteenth-birthday party in Havana a short while before, hopes she can salvage it, hide it from her mother.

When her mother leaves the room, Mumín stands alone at the window. Her hair is twisted into a French braid. She has the sweetness of the young Natasha in *War and Peace*. It's hard to describe the turmoil inside her. She wishes, for a moment, to be with Naty in Havana. We had tried to phone Havana earlier but couldn't get the call through, not on New Year's Eve. Exhausted, on the verge of tears, Alina's daughter turns out the light and goes to sleep.

On January 1, 1994, Mumín awakens in the United States. It is a hundred years since Great-grandfather Herbert Clews sailed from England to secure his future in Cuba.

CHAPTER 7

A Family in Splinters

January 1994. Two weeks after visiting Columbus, I was back in Havana, carrying with me the pictures I'd taken at Elena's house: Alina clowning in her "escape" wig, Mumín talking to reporters, the champagne gala on New Year's Eve. But for Naty and her mother, it was too soon—or perhaps too difficult—to contemplate the perilous, unfamiliar landscape in which Alina was apparently thriving. Still caught in Alina's whirlwind, Doña Natica and Naty were like tornado victims struggling to make sense of the twister's damage. Although they had expressed conflicting reactions to Alina's disappearance, both women came together in a determination to figure out how, suddenly, without warning, the family had found itself in splinters.

For Naty, Mumín's sixteenth-birthday party marked the start of Alina's odyssey. Celebrated at Naty's house, on the night before her daughter's secret flight to Madrid, this year's party was particularly festive. Alina, with her black-market connections, had provided the sodas, the miniature frankfurters, the delicately iced white cake. So many of Mumín's school friends came, as did her own father. He had danced with his daughter all night, whirling her around the room as though she were his partner in a comic pas de deux, a wild, laughing afternoon of a faun.

For some time, Naty had longed to see more of this irreverent, playful side of her granddaughter. She had, in truth, been worried that Mumín might enter the convent. Since her christening, the Roman Church had enchanted the girl: the Virgen del Cobre; the fragrant smell of incense; the sound of the Communion bell; the peace. But now, Naty thought, she wouldn't lose her granddaughter to the bishops. It never crossed her mind that she was about to lose Alina instead—and not to the Church.

On the following day, a friend of Naty's called to say that she'd heard the radio announce Alina's arrival in Madrid. Not surprisingly, Naty's immediate reaction was denial. A short-circuiting of that symbiotic connection with Alina was too threatening to contemplate. (But she told me that she had noted it was odd that Alina's keys—and even the car registration—had been abandoned on the front-hall table. Even Mumín, who insisted that her mother was resting at home, couldn't explain why Alina hadn't taken the keys.) To anyone who called, Naty insisted that her daughter was asleep in her own bed—but she didn't cross the street to ring Alina's doorbell. "Well," she thought, "it's not my daughter who's left the country. Fidel must have another daughter. Who knows how many daughters he's had?"

So many rumors. The talk about Alina was always filling the air. Some said she had threatened to leave on a leaky raft, or to hide at the bottom of a trunk, like a stowaway. Fueling the talk, Alina had agreed to frequent interviews about her desperate straits, her impatience with fate. She had often said: "I must get out of this country. Here, I'm just growing old. What will become of me when I'm fifty?" But nothing came of her Houdini-like schemes.

With Alina's impudence—nobody else in Cuba called Fidel an assassin publicly—her sense of irony, her self-deprecating humor, she had turned her ambiguous position into a profession of sorts. "My father's island is nothing but an enormous prison." She was a master at calling attention to herself, at straining for dramatic effect. But she didn't realize that this persistent focus on her father made sense only in Cuba, not in Spain or anywhere else.

Alina had posed for foreign photographers and denounced her father on the terraces of so many of his tourist hotels. Sometimes, she borrowed the moral high ground. "I'm concerned about the country's moral decline. The people are ready to kill each other for a bicycle." At other times, when the more sentimental writers seemed to want it, she played the part of a frail, endearing match girl. "Cheese. Today, I will have only a little bit of cheese to eat." To the practical Naty, it seemed that Alina should make the most of her situation with the press, because she could never leave the island. She found the clamor about Alina's bolting completely unreal—foolish, too.

So different from her daughter, Doña Natica knew at once that Alina had gone. Naty remembered her mother's words: trembling, thick with fear. She told me that the anguished woman had been listening to Miami's Radio Martí, when she heard an announcement—incorrect, as it turned out—that Fidel Castro's daughter had escaped to the mainland in a small boat. The station warned its listeners to be careful when boarding their own freedom rafts: the *balseros* were drowning, and sharks were feeding on their drifting bodies. Doña Natica told her daughter that she had had a vision of Alina floating in a watery grave.

When she told me the real story, Doña Natica cried harder, more plaintively. In front of me, at least, she had often worn an elaborate, brightly painted tragic mask. Not that her grief wasn't authentic, but she liked to present it as a piece of theatre—a drama in which she played the suffering heroine. But now her words had an added edge. Folded into Doña Natica's sorrow there was an unspoken anger at Naty for the loss of yet another granddaughter: "We have been left alone, but, fortunately, I won't live very long. Once again, I'm experiencing the pain of Nina's leaving. I thought I wouldn't see my eldest granddaughter again. And it's true; I never did."

May 1995. By meeting Nina Fernández Burton, Naty's elder daughter, I thought I could complete the family portrait. Nina's life, I knew, was shaped by her exile from Cuba, the single event that had shattered her grandmother. Doña Natica, I knew, thought that Nina was suffering the effects of a violent separation from her Cuban inheritance. But from my conversations with Nina, I was confident that the figures from her past were no more than blurred figures in an altered inner landscape. At Nina's invitation—and to see if I was right—I traveled to Sparksburg, Illinois, the town where she lives with her second husband, Ted, and her son, Peter.

An energetic woman in her late forties, Nina has the large, generous nature of someone favored by good fortune—someone wise enough to know it might have been otherwise. Although her shining black hair and dark almond eyes reflect her ancestry, Nina never thinks about Cuba, and would never return, even for a visit. Whether Fidel Castro remains there or not is a matter of indifference to all three members of the Burton family. The blessing of her life, Nina would argue, is that it brings her peace. When Peter brings his friends home, they laugh about his mother's tidiness, her obsessive need for order.

Nina teaches Spanish at the high school. Unsettled by change, she relishes repetitions: *"Yo canto, tú cantas, él canta. . . . Repite,*

repite. Yo canto, tú cantas, él canta." ("I sing, you sing, he sings. . . . Repeat, repeat. I sing, you sing, he sings.") Several times a week, she leads a class in aerobics. "And one, and two. . . . And again, and one and two . . ." Strong, commanding as she does her leg lifts, Nina feels the pleasure of the class as it moves to the repeated, expected beat of her music.

Nina and Ted never entertain, nor do they have dinner with friends. Sitting in the living room or waiting in a restaurant makes them both fidget. Ted would rather be in the garage tinkering with his car. Nina laughs. "Peter can't believe it. Whenever he calls, we're here. I can't remember the last time I saw eleven o'clock. Even on weekends, the mall closes at nine, and that's as late as we're out, ever." She continues: "Sometimes when we're home, we take the phone into the garden, so that we can hear it ring in case Peter is trying to reach us." Peter is the stillpoint in Nina's slowly turning world. Whenever he's gone, she makes a deal with God: "Bring Peter home safely and I'll go to church for five hundred Sundays in a row. Anything. Just bring him home."

Nina's life might be thought predictable, even somewhat banal, but not by her. "I like to wake up in the morning and know exactly what I'm going to do. My life works. I've had the best father and son. Ted and I love each other. We wouldn't change a thing." On the wall, Nina has framed the certificate admitting Peter to the United States Air Force Academy. She's proud of her tall, blond, patriot son. Could Peter's friends imagine that his grandmother was once Fidel Castro's lover?

NINA is anxious to talk about her mother's visit in the spring of 1982. When Naty Revuelta came to see Nina in Illinois, it was because this vilified mother wanted to explain to her daughter that she had never abandoned her. After listening to Naty's story, Nina confronted her father: "Is this what really happened? Did my mother believe you'd taken me only for a visit? Had you agreed to return me to her in nine months, after the school term ended?" Crying, Orlando admitted that he'd fled to the States with no intention of ever returning Nina to Naty. He had lied to Nina, allowed her to believe that she couldn't go home because her mother didn't want her.

The practical Nina, however, couldn't remain angry at her adored father. She immediately forgave him—the man who had lost his wife, a medical practice, and his country. He had struggled hard to make a home for his daughter. After landing in Miami with Nina—it was the summer of 1961—a bewildered Orlando had gone to a department store and bought two complete place settings of Wedgwood china and two crystal goblets so that he and his daughter could eat dinner at home. Neither of them had ever been to a market, or had an instinct for cooking. Onto the Wedgwood dinner plates, with their delicate blue borders, Orlando ladled canned black beans.

Terrified that, in Miami, his daughter might be kidnapped and sent back to Havana, Orlando settled in a small town as far from South Florida as his medical skills could take him. It was hard for a man his age to retrain in a foreign language, to start a second career as a doctor; but Orlando succeeded. At night, he worked at a veterans' hospital just outside Sparksburg. He caught a few hours of sleep in a wooden chair while Nina slumbered on in the bed provided for the overworked residents. "I'm very grateful to him," says Nina. "But it's what I would have done for my own child."

Of his daughter, Orlando asked very little—only that she not dress in red or black, that she not wear a turban. He wanted to erase those few reminders of Naty.

NINA'S own brush with passion filled her with sympathy for her mother. During her first marriage—to a born-again Christian, an expert in security systems—a neighbor had looked at her, desire in his eyes, and she had returned his glance. Shortly after, she had an affair with him and separated from her husband. For the following three years, Nina angered her father, confused her friends, and compromised her home. From the experience came a terrible knowledge that she shared with her mother. The Cubans would have put it like this: *Nadie coge mariposa sin mancharse las manos.* (You can't catch a butterfly without staining your hands.)

The experience left Nina feeling more compassion for her mother than had most of Naty's Havana friends, something that must have surprised Orlando. At their 1992 reunion, Naty had listened to her daughter's own story of romantic obsession and observed: *"Te puso en el bolsillo, igual que Fidel."* ("He put you in his pocket. That's what happened to me with Fidel.") In that moment, their common experience created a magnetic field that held mother and daughter together. "You have to have had the experience to understand," Nina said. "It's worth it. Everything is like the high sound on a string guitar."

Nina left her dutiful first husband, and committed herself to an irresponsible lover. The plot might have been the brainchild of any soap-opera writer. "I took one look at him and that was it. Nothing mattered but the moments I had with him. My father had me followed," Nina continued. "He didn't believe that I was at the drawing center every evening. Who goes to art classes when it's almost midnight?

"But I couldn't function without this difficult, selfish man. Nothing had a reality but the time we had together. I'd go to a restaurant and order what he wanted, not what I liked, just to feel close to him. It made me understand my mother, and how she was willing to gamble everything for the love of Fidel." A Cuban *bolero*, popular in the fifties, came to mind: *"Todo una vida, me estaría contigo, no me importa en que forma, ni como, ni donde, pero junto a tí."* ("All my life, I would be with you. It doesn't matter how or where or when, but only that we're together.")

Nina might have continued to be a source of comfort to her mother, but their lives diverged again. After Naty's return, she never wrote to her daughter. It was too strenuous; so much experience separated them. Naty couldn't imagine teaching aerobics to women in pony tails, running shoes, and sweat pants; Nina, after leaving Havana, had never again seen a ration card or worried about filling the car with gas. What did they have in common? Besides, Nina doesn't like to confide in women and has never trusted them. She made it clear to me that she is grateful to have a son: "I'm so glad I have Peter. I wouldn't have wanted a daughter, I would have feared never being close to her."

But it was more than that. I thought that, with Nina, Naty feared that she was walking in a minefield. A careless story about Orlando, the wrong mention of Fidel—who knew if there weren't buried negative feelings that would be roused in her daughter? It just wasn't worth it.

WHEN Nina talks about her mother now, she's unsentimental. If Naty wanted her forgiveness, she had it. But that didn't mean that she could be part of the family. For that, she would have to have a stake in Nina's present life. And Naty couldn't even imagine Nina's life: the drives to the shopping mall; her worries about Ted's smoking; the teachers' room at the high school where she has lunch with her friends; Ted and Peter having breakfast together; listening to Phil Collins on the kitchen radio. Naty didn't even know Peter, probably wouldn't ever meet his children.

The two women are strangers to each other. Nothing can be done about that. Nina even has trouble retrieving memories of Naty. Two images linger in her mind: In one, her mother is putting on a bright-red dress, because she and Nina's father are going out for dinner. The telephone rings. Orlando has to cancel their plans—a patient needs him at the clinic. Nina remembers her mother on that evening, a pensive, beautiful woman in a red silk dress with no place to go. The second image is of the farewell at the airport when Nina was not yet twelve—her mother waving, Nina's own nine fingers in the air counting the number of months she'd be away. She recalls the moment of leaving, Doña Natica crying—the noise of the airplane engines.

Now Nina never travels, not even to Springfield, the state capital, an hour away. Nor is her curiosity about Alina, who has been in Columbus, Georgia, for more than a year, strong enough to set Nina in motion. Unmotivated, absorbed in her family's present, she makes no plans to see her sister. Anyway, it's more than likely that Alina has no interest in a reunion with Nina. What would they say to each other? Nina, who can't even remember Havana, last saw her sister when Alina was four. "I don't know what I could offer her. Our lives are so different. How will she survive? How can she go to the dentist if she hasn't any health insurance?"

As I leave, Nina's final words are about her mother. "What's past is past," she says. "I feel sorry for my mother because she's paid an enormous price—and for nothing. She's lost her daughters, her grandchildren. That's life. It goes on. You get on the train or you're lost."

October 1995. Fidel Castro was coming to New York to attend the fiftieth-anniversary salute to the United Nations. A group of right-wing Cuban exiles invited Alina to New York to lead a demonstration against her father's five-day visit. Still living in Columbus, Georgia, she was delighted at the prospect. Like many people, Alina looked forward to the intense rush that New York City promised everyone. And there was more. Even for a metropolis that took most events in its stride, the UN's celebration would be an overwhelming event: white tents at the entrance to the Secretariat to welcome most of the world's leaders; Fidel Castro and the other heads of state would walk on red carpets past white-gloved honor guards.

If it was strange to have Fidel in New York, it would be stranger still for me to have Alina in my city. We hadn't seen each other since that New Year's Eve nearly two years ago. Knowing that she no longer wanted me around, I had returned to my house on New Year's Day. My dominant memories of the few days I had spent with her were of her angry, shifting moods: she wouldn't receive Osvaldo Rodríguez, her angel; another childhood friend, Ramiro Fernández, was banished because he was a photographer. My sense then had been that Alina had conflicting impulses towards me—on the one hand to court me, on the other to see me gone.

Nor had I been shocked by that eccentric behavior. In Havana, I had observed Alina turning away from her friends, even her family. Was it out of some half-formed fear of being used? Sometimes, for example, she found the prospect of my writing threatening to her; at other times she seemed to seek the added attention. Having signed her own contract with a German publisher, Alina would brook no competition. Yet she often seemed convinced that my portrait of her family would bear little resemblance to her own story, and, indeed, that it might make the public even more interested in her autobiography. In any case, it was clear that, more often than not, Alina didn't want to talk to me in Columbus, and I had been relieved to move on.

Contemplating Alina's arrival in New York, I was confident of at least one thing. She was furious at her mother for allowing me to use her photographs and particularly her correspondence with Fidel, even though she was free to use the letters herself. To Alina, it seemed disloyal, something akin to Naty's having taken in her husband, Mumín's father, after the couple had separated.

I thought about my own situation with Naty—and my awareness that she was the victim of opposing pulls. Having her story in print, a means of recovering her romance, was of enormous importance to her. At the same time, however, she had maternal feelings that argued in favor of meeting Alina's emotional demands.

Nothing was resolved. Between my anger—they, after all, had wanted me to write their story—and the enormous guilt that made Naty ambivalent, we both found it uncomfortable to touch on the progress of the book. We took to exchanging small presents instead: a book on Cuban painting, scented bath oils, a silk blouse, a recipe for *dulce de leche,* a bottle of Florida cologne. (But once I did receive a postcard from Naty with a proposed title for the book. *Royal Flush,* she wanted to call it.)

Alina's coming filled me with anxiety, even though things were better between us. A few months earlier, during the summer of 1995, I had received a call from a friend of Naty's asking me to tell Alina that her mother was in the hospital for minor surgery. So much time had gone by, I didn't expect that we would have a rapprochement. But when I called Alina, she was as friendly as if nothing had ever happened.

Alina and I continued our conversations. In these calls—and later, in face-to-face meetings in New York—she was increasingly eager to talk about what had happened to her. First her media attention had subsided; and then it was over. She had noticed that, when she couldn't keep feeding the piranhas, they lost interest in her. Constantly asked about her father, she had recited the same litany of sins: he was a brutal dictator, his country could only be described as a prison. Pressed for an intimate portrait of Fidel, she ran out of lines. What did he eat for breakfast? Did he love his children? Had he loved her mother? The questions reminded her how little she knew about him.

In Havana, everyone had looked out for her. With her mother's protection, Alina had lived on her own terms: she flirted with the press when she wanted to, ignored it when it inconvenienced her. At home, she could make a full-time profession of being Castro's daughter. She could play her like Cassandra, an oracle reading the future, or Rapunzel, the maiden locked inside a tower. Given the absence of possibilities on the island, it was natural to find Alina acting in this never-ending drama of her father's which held the Cubans captive.

The same conditions didn't exist here. This country didn't focus exclusively on Cuba; the role of Fidel's daughter was no more than a bit part. Yet, without that former self-definition, who could Alina be? She traveled abroad, bought lots of clothes, tried to write; but nothing seemed to work. Once a skillful, defensive driver, she couldn't even pass the state road test in Georgia.

Sometimes Alina watched television in order to learn English, or ventured out with Elena to the stores at the Peachtree Mall. What was she to do with all the designer clothes—the Calvin Kleins, the Escada suits, the Prada handbag? Cinderella in her ball dress when the coach failed to come couldn't have been more forlorn.

WHEN Alina arrived in New York—even before she entered the city—the afternoon tabloid featured her picture on its front page. In the wake of recovered celebrity, she revived. A drumbeat of questions rolled over her: Would she see her father? Was she planning to give interviews? Would Fidel topple from power? When she reached her destination, the police wanted to know where she would be demonstrating, so that they could protect her.

At the corner of First Avenue and East Forty-seventh Street, thousands of protesters—some from countries so obscure and impoverished that their leaders rode to the United Nation on the subway—opened a Pandora's box of resentments: Africans protested against Zaire's Mobutu, human-rights activists demanded fair treatment for the Tamils, Indians pleaded for justice from Pakistan's Benazir Bhutto. A confident Fidel Castro, in an unexpectedly well-tailored dark-blue suit, delivered a speech on social justice.

Fidel's presence in New York brought Alina back to life: "I hope nothing happens to my father," she told me laughingly. I was reminded that she loved to clown. "Where would I be without him?" For the demonstrations, Alina painted on a stage face. She wore her most theatrical cosmetics—a wine-brown color on her stenciled mouth, kohl on the lids of her dark eyes. The heavy, unforgiving makeup did its best to hide her natural doelike beauty. She was Queen Esther pleading for her people, Evita Perón blowing kisses into the crowds of *descamisados*.

This drama was the tie to her father. Over and over again, she turned to him in her thoughts, sometimes holding imaginary conversations with him. Whenever we talked, I could see how much she longed for a more ordinary connection with him. She could never let go of that fantasy. But not even a family album with photographs of father and daughter existed. Alina riding a pony with her brother Fidelito; Alina at the edge of the water, Fidel hovering behind her—these sweet scenes weren't even phantom memories for Alina.

Listening to the crowd roar, she was the dictator's child again. *"¡Viva Alina!"* shouted the demonstrators. *"¡Viva Alina!"* When Fidel passed in front of her, Alina thought she had caught his glance. But he walked right past his chanting daughter, didn't see her—saw, instead, himself, more than three decades ago, when he had captured the city with his fierce, bold presence. At the Abyssinian Baptist Church in Harlem, he would wear his green fatigues and take in the cheers of the congregation. ("Fidel, Fidel, Fidel," they roared.) But here, at the United Nations, he complained to an aide, he'd received only "an atom of President Clinton's sight." Fidel's distorting mirror reflected, like Alina's, nothing but confusing self-images.

Later, when he attended a private reception, hosted by a well-known magazine publisher, he was treated as a friendly dinosaur. He defended the absence of free elections—a "popularity competition" between "demagogues and liars." He gave his views on heaven and hell. (An Islamic heaven, with sex, he said, was preferable to its puritanical Christian equivalent.) His own selection as head of state he likened to the process through which the College of Cardinals elects a pope. "The eyes of a killer shark," a guest said of him; "there's no emotion behind them."

Fidel expressed no sense of responsibility for Cuba's fate, no rage, no disappointment with himself. He failed to consider that he was to blame for selling his country down the Soviet river. At a meeting in the Time & Life Building, he spoke about the 1962 Missile Crisis as though it had just taken place. Sometimes, Fidel seemed to live in his own reconstructions of the past; that accounted for his endless speeches, his self-absorption, his passion for his own words, their created realities.

On CNN, Fidel refused to discuss Alina: "You have raised a question about a personal subject—a very delicate question. It seems to me that I should not touch upon it in public," he said. "I wouldn't be acting like a gentleman if I did." Never before had Fidel mentioned Alina in a speech. He had never acknowledged, even this implicitly, that he was her father. ("It was important," Naty said later. "He could have denied her.")

For Alina, this painted, insecure child, Fidel's comments had amounted to a father's embrace. On television, he had seemed distant, but Alina (who believes in telepathy) thought that he had been talking to her. She thought he was telling her how to behave so that he could be proud of her.

ALINA hadn't found a balance. In New York, she was uncertain in her movements, as though her brain were startled, overwhelmed with confusion. It accounted for some of her awkwardness, her failure to monitor an often devilish behavior. At dinner with a friend of mine, a prominent oncologist, I listened to her rail against the nonsmoking rule in the restaurant. If they wouldn't let her smoke, then we'd all have to go somewhere else. On the following day, she called the doctor at his office. Would he leave his patients, take some time off to help her move? She had decided that she might want to take an apartment in Queens.

Meeting with Lincoln Díaz-Balart, the conservative Florida congressman, Alina mentioned changing her surname to Castro. Wouldn't it be a better name to use on the Phil Donahue show? What would she wear? (Could she trust Díaz-Balart, whose Aunt Mirta, Fidel's ex-wife, so hated Naty?) She was being photographed by *Harper's Bazaar*. They suggested that she pose draped around the Statue of Liberty. Shouldn't she have been allowed to keep the smart black jacket from Dolce and Gabbana? Yes, that was important.

November 1995. Flying to Washington, D.C., from La Guardia Airport, Alina didn't have to produce photo identification, because the ticket agent recognized her as Fidel Castro's daughter. When we boarded the plane, she said: "In Havana, I gave myself over to being his daughter but it didn't change my life. Here, it matters a lot that I'm his child."

Alina endured, at times, great confusion about her identity; scared, apprehensive, she had a need to defend herself that made her hostile. Speaking to members of a conservative Washington foundation, she resisted their generous offers to get her book-in-progress published. Suspicions clouded her judgment. "Why should I cooperate with them? Anyway, I haven't time to think about the book. I'm much too busy."

(She already had the contract with the German book publisher, but believed that they were afraid to publish her submitted manuscript. Could she really have thought—when she talked to me, she seemed so certain—that her father's agents had burned her German editor's house and car?)

As we were leaving, the foundation's president gave her a copy of their report on the activities of her father's infamous Ministry of the Interior. On the cover, she scribbled: "Chanel, Charivari, Escada dress and jacket." She laughed. *"¡Mira! el Ministerio se convierte a casa de modas."* ("Look! The Ministry of the Interior has turned into a house of fashion.")

WHEN Fidel Castro returned to Havana, Alina remained in New York at the Metropolitan Club. She had been staying with Elena Amos, who had come to town for the demonstrations. But with Elena, things had gone badly. Alina's new imagining of the world didn't include following her benefactor home. "I won't go back to Columbus, Georgia," she told me. "Elena is going to have to get in touch with the new me." They wouldn't see each other again.

They were shopping at Henri Bendel's when everything came to a crisis. Alina's patron had refused to indulge her in still more expensive clothes. Alina liked to test Elena, to measure devotion in spent dollars, to find out whether she was loved enough to be given everything she wanted. "I think Elena's mad at me," she said. "I told her that her Cubans didn't love her. They just wanted her money." Alina was furious with Orestes Lorenzo, the decorated aviator whom Elena adored. "He's gotten a great car—a Lexus. She's rented a plane for him, even a house. Why does he deserve all that? What have I gotten from her? I'm finished with Elena Amos." Freedom, the intoxication of absolute freedom—that's what she felt.

But though she wanted to be free, Alina, anxious about her own self-presentation, was searching for a sophisticated guide to living in New York. When I introduced her to Nelia Barletta de Cates, she thought she'd found deliverance. Nelia's extraordinary presence—tall, high-cheekboned, fashionably silver-haired—was at once dazzling and beguiling. (Alina wanted the surface glamour of Nelia's life, commuting between houses in New York, Paris, and the Bahamas.) But for Alina, Nelia advised getting a job. Though born to great wealth in Cuba, Nelia understood the rules of survival: "Play the hand you're dealt. It's the only one you have. When you haven't any money, it doesn't matter who you are, you have to work. Haven't we all seen *Casablanca*?" After Nelia's words, Alina seemed to lose all interest in having her as a patron. They never saw each other again.

From New York, Alina believed she was charting a new course, but it didn't seem so to me. With everyone she courted, the pattern seemed to be the same: infatuation, disillusionment, abandonment. The periods of her life—the time of her marriages, for example—were marked by sudden, swift splits. Her self-destructive energy seemed to vent itself in malice, in exaggerations and cruelty. But when her actions hurt someone, she appeared to have no sense of the reality of that person's pain, no notion that it would linger. After her break with Elena Amos, Alina called her again as though nothing had happened. Hearing her voice, Elena had simply put down the telephone: "Alina, *adiós*." That's all she'd said.

From the library in my house, Alina called Mumín to tell her she wasn't going back to Columbus. Having children of my own, I found it chilling to watch. But even as I heard her ordering Mumín to sell the furniture and leave the apartment, I sensed that Alina didn't think she might be causing her daughter some distress.

Fortunately, I thought, Mumín was self-reliant. In this country, she had fared better than Alina. She had made friends, learned to speak English, and become a member of the National Honor Society. A high-school senior, she was coping alone with college entrance exams, with homework, with camping trips. Had her mother's plans not changed, and had Mumín remained in Columbus, she would have graduated from Cardinal Pacelli High School in the spring. Her success was no accident, for Mumín invited warm feelings.

She adored her mother. But it wouldn't have made sense to count on someone who couldn't deal with things, who often slammed the telephone down at the slightest provocation.

It was an awkward moment. After her mother's call, Mumín packed her suitcase, closed the door, and drove over to Elena Amos's house. Tired of problems, Elena, meanwhile, had retreated inside herself. Though she loved Mumín—indeed, admired her—this kindly woman wasn't prepared to take her in for the rest of the school year. She could let go of the teenager. Her family urged Elena to send Mumín to her father in Miami.

Naty was poised to step into the breach. In a coincidence that seems incredible to me because she traveled so rarely, she happened to be visiting a friend in West Palm Beach. Receiving word that Elena wanted her to make the plans for Mumín's departure, she arranged to fetch her granddaughter. On the next morning, Naty (who hadn't seen either of her daughters on this visit) boarded Elena's private plane for the flight to Columbus.

It was a familiar position. When Mumín had been about to leave Cuba, Naty had met with Fidel, in the Presidential Palace, to make the arrangements for their grandchild's trip. He had insisted that Mumín be accompanied on her flight. "We're not going to send her alone," he had told Naty, "as though she were a package." Since Naty wouldn't go, because she feared being chased by the press in Miami, Mumín's father was the obvious candidate. But would he return to Cuba? She had vouched for the dancer. He had promised her that he would go right back to Havana—and then he'd broken his word.

In Columbus, Naty folded Mumín's clothes—Alina didn't want her things—packing them into large duffel bags. She noticed that Alina's sweaters still had price tags hanging from the labels. Her daughter never even looked at what she bought, but Naty saved everything: string, rubber bands, a favorite worn bathrobe, battered suitcases. When she finished cleaning out the small flat, she took her granddaughter by the hand and flew to Miami.

Naty's most passionate feelings were now for Mumín. Before visiting me for several days a week or so later, she made sure that Mumín had settled in with her father and his new wife.

I couldn't but observe that this young woman had rescued her grandmother from the past. She had carried her into the present, where, for the first time, Naty became a mother, felt motherhood's powerful impulse, breathed its hidden pleasures.

January 1996. Suddenly Naty was in Greenwich Village. In Havana, she was an insider—or so I thought. Through the intrigue, the complications in her country's history, she had moved confidently—maintaining extinct routines for her demanding mother, seeing to tangled family matters. That's why it came as a surprise to me, seeing her in New York City, to meet a woman so unlike the one I'd known in Cuba. Here, where Naty was a stranger, there was a lightness about her. Without the burdens of her household, free of Alina's recriminations, the elusive Naty came forth—Manolo Revuelta's romantic daughter, who took pleasure in music, in art, in good company.

Certainly it was a long time coming. So intent on understanding Naty's fascination with Fidel, I had failed to see how much her emotional posture had to do with pleasing her mother. Doña Natica's expectation of her daughter, from the time she was a child, was that Naty serve her. In Havana, Naty had for decades been her mother's chambermaid.

Now, in New York, her spirits soaring, she seemed free of the effects of that indenture—but at moments only. She reminded me of a little bird I once saw in a market in New Delhi. When a miniature gate opened, it flew out of its bamboo cage—but then right back in again. I guess, for some people, it isn't bearable to live with complete freedom.

The New-York Historical Society was having a small exhibition of the pottery made by Doña Natica's ancestors—it was the first place in the city that Naty wanted to go. Not convinced by the idea of self-invention, Naty believed, instead, that inheritance could determine the boundaries of a personal destiny. That's why she was so interested in her descent from James Clews, the English potter who made a pilgrimage into the Indiana frontier, built his own kiln, and started a profitable business. (The deep, rich coloring of his underglaze printing was said to be unsurpassed by any other manufacturer of his day.) Naty lingered in front of the most original of James's pieces, *The Landing of Lafayette*. She told me it made her think that she should have become an artist. It gave her a sense of the importance of unraveling the tale of her family's diaspora.

A COMPLICATED woman, harder to read than the rest of her family, Naty aroused my anger whenever we talked about her daughters. With my own emotions rising to the surface, I lost my original sympathy for her. It wasn't Naty's fault, not the anger. It was that a buried, infantile rage at my own mother for leaving me had become inextricable from a rising, uncontainable anger at Naty.

I had to watch out. Naty wasn't my mother. But I had gathered rage and placed it on her shoulders. From the time I was a child, whenever I'd asked my own mother why she had abandoned me, she had answered with a rash of self-justifications. If she couldn't be with me, it was because she loved me too much.

How this reminded me of Naty's remarks about Nina. It had infuriated me that, when she had taken her leave of Nina in 1960 (then rarely bothered to write), she had insisted that everything was Orlando's fault. And what about Alina? Hadn't she been born to further her mother's ambitions? Alina had been a sacrifice—a child that I thought had been conceived in order to get Fidel's attention. Hidden in that story, and this was the source of my rage, I thought I had found something of my own.

Once I figured this out, my anger began to dissolve. Suddenly I recovered my affection for Naty—a woman with whom I could have an espresso, a conversation about a painting, a lunch in SoHo. In West Palm Beach, at the huge shopping malls, she told me that she had become disoriented, but not here in New York. Wearing a flowing cashmere scarf that touched the hem of her long white wool dress, Naty strolled the streets like a confident film star—Greta Garbo striding along East Fifty-second Street, Josephine Baker walking her cheetah along Park Avenue.

Without the rage, I could accept that, throughout her life, two incompatible forces existed inside her in an uneasy truce. Now that she was seventy, there was a reconciliation. In her love for Mumín, Naty fused passion and reason, creating out of these opposing energies a single, profound maternal feeling.

I HAD thought of bringing the two women together. Whenever Naty talked about missing Alina, whom she hadn't seen for two years, there was a look of pain in her face. And so I called Alina, who was now living in Queens, and asked her to dinner with her mother. Because we had invited Ed Goodman and his wife, Lorna, it seemed particularly appropriate. (Ed Goodman, Nena Mañach Goodman's son, is also the nephew of Jorge Mañach, a distinguished Harvard-educated professor who once supported Fidel and later became disillusioned with the revolutionary leader's politics.)

We often have dinner with Ed and Lorna, but Naty's presence made everyone more self-conscious, and more attentive. The dinner coincided with the end of Naty's visit, one that had given her some liberation from her troubles with her mother.

(Doña Natica wasn't here—of course, she'd have been thrilled to meet Nena's son.) Naty's visit to New York had made her savor pleasures she'd almost forgotten. I reminded her that she was once the toast of Havana—and could be again.

"Havana is a scorched city," Naty said, "but it will come back. When it does, you must visit me." Graciously, she promised to give Ed a painting by one of his Mañach cousins. "I meant to bring it with me from Havana," she announced. Maybe this was a dinner of reconciliations—personal, but political too. If Nena Mañach's son and Doña Natica's daughter could come together for a candlelit dinner in New York City, things might be returning to normal.

Naty's light and amusing anecdotes provided the tone for the evening. Naty described French surrealist André Breton riding on a bus in Havana. A mariachi band climbed on and started to play. Three nuns in white habits got up from their seats and began to dance in the aisles. Said Breton: *"Ce pays est vraiment trop surréaliste pour y habiter."* ("This country is just too surreal to inhabit.") The stories went on and on: Enrico Caruso, costumed in a long skirt and lady's wig, being chased through the streets of Havana by a nonoperatic policeman who thought he was impersonating a woman; the Caballero de Paris roaming the streets in his black cape, gallantly offering his "celestial army" to anyone who needed it. When the evening ended, nobody mentioned Fidel.

When the doorbell rang, we were still seated in the dining room. Alina, who had declined my invitation, arrived with her friend James, a tall young man, Irish, wrapped in an enormous camel-colored coat. "When I came from Cuba," she had said, "I consulted an astrologer who told me that I would spend two difficult years in the South, and then my life would change for the better. My mother is the past, not the present. I have to separate myself from her."

They must have wanted a more intimate reunion; it had been two years since they had seen each other. But that didn't seem to be the case; there was too much of a strain between them. Alina stared at her mother, whom she hadn't embraced, and focused on her necklace. "I like your necklace. Why don't you give it to me?" A flustered Naty removed the necklace of flattened gold squares and handed it to her daughter.

To break the silence, I asked Alina to tell us about her work with the Cuban-American exiles. "My father's right about these exile groups," she said. "The people in them are impossible. Imagine, they offered me the key to Perth Amboy when the one I wanted was to New York. In any case, I won't be here long. I'm off to meet the Queen of Spain. . . ." Naty recovered herself, smiled: "Isn't Alina clever?" she said. "While everyone's still looking for the flour, Alina has already made biscuits."

They must leave, Alina announced shortly. "My James has commitments, an important engagement." Nervous, her face pale, she said in a burst of English, "I transcend!" Turning to look at her mother, Alina got up from the table and, with relish, repeated her New Age phrase: "I transcend!" She tried to measure the effect of her words on the guests. Had she said something memorable?

After Alina went home, Naty took the abandoned necklace from the table and put it around her neck. She was relieved to possess it again. The following day, Alina returned. "My mother offered me the necklace," she told me, "but then she took it back." Suddenly Alina reminded me of a porcelain ballerina in a glass case that I was given as a little girl. The figure pirouetted on her toes, but only when someone came to wind her. Untouched, unattended, the dancer never moved. "I'd like to find myself in Havana," Alina said, "having to escape again. In fact, what I like best is a fast game of cat-and-mouse with my father."

On Naty's last night in New York, we saw *Sunset Boulevard*. Alone in her Hollywood palace, descending her grand staircase, the aging Norma Desmond makes her customary entrance into the past. "I was big," she says, "it's the pictures that got small." Even at the end, when the police take her away on a murder charge, Norma still believes that she's a great star whose fans are clamoring for her.

Who else sustains the illusion that time has stopped? I remembered being told by a CBS reporter that, during his recent stay in New York, Fidel had revisited the Hotel Theresa in Harlem. How the crowds had cheered him when he'd stayed there in 1960! Now the hotel had become an office building, and there was no one to greet him. When the Cuban leader stepped from his car and raised his right arm, he didn't know that he was waving at ghosts. As we were leaving the theatre, Naty turned to me and said, "That's who Fidel is, he's Norma Desmond."

EPILOGUE

WHEN I was a little girl, my grandmother and I often sailed from Miami to Havana on the SS *Florida,* one of the efficient steamers that dutifully ferried travelers across the narrow straits. In the comfort and security of one of those journeys, an elderly gentleman who carried a silver cane told me a story that really frightened me. It was, it turns out, a cautionary tale about exile.

On June 29, 1856, Señor Matías Pérez, an enterprising manufacturer of umbrella awnings, set out to impress the people of Havana. While thousands looked on in awe, he boarded an air balloon, ascended into the clouds, and disappeared from Cuba, forever. When the old man recounted the tale, my grandmother laughed, but I was suddenly terrified. Imagine: a man floats into the clouds in a balloon, looks down, sees the people becoming smaller and smaller, realizes that he is alone, never to see his family, his friends, or his country again.

Sometimes I have puzzled over whether Alina and Mumín, leaving Havana behind, uncertain that they might ever return, felt as lost as the vanishing balloonist. Suddenly lifted out of their own spot on the earth, the two women arrived in a place that was utterly strange, entirely unfamiliar. Perhaps Doña

Natica and Naty, stranded on their island, suffered as jagged a disconnection from their previous worlds as did Alina, Mumín, and the formidable Señor Matías Pérez.

From Havana to Miami—in fact, all across Cuba and the United States—the stories multiply of families separated from each other by a stretch of water that governments have made treacherous. It's hard to conceive of political ideologies so brilliant, so radiant that they're worth all the human suffering they've created. And what has been achieved? It's probable that the real legacy of the Cuban Revolution is little more than estrangement, brutality, self-delusion, and the pain of exile.

NOT SO long ago, when I could still board a Miami flight to Havana, I had to get myself to the airport before sunrise. Then long lines, travel documents, visa forms, officious clerks. After the hassles, the silence—the stillness—of the terminal was surreal. An air of mystery, a hint of the furtive, pervaded the corridors; the airport itself was still sleeping, its restaurants were closed, its newsstands were covered with iron grates.

A baggage handler—an overweight, nervous man in his late fifties—offered to wheel my suitcase to the airline counter. The moment I agreed, he revealed himself as Cuban, handing me photographs of his son Jorge, a slim, laughing young man sitting on a motorcycle, and of his mother, Edelmira. She was a stout woman in a green sundress, a delicate, gold chain around her freckled throat. His older brother, Juan, who had fought for Fidel in the mountains, had languished in jail for fifteen years. There was no photograph of Juan, his mother's favorite.

The man was persistent, struggling against my weary indifference. It was irritating to have to know about his friends and relatives in Cuba. But that wasn't all: he then had to make sure I understood that he wasn't really a porter; he was the manager of a sugar plantation who still worried about the harvest. Someone in his family had married a member of the Nuñez del Castillo family. Did I know who they were? He would tell me, of course.

The baggage handler was a man in exile—a man floating higher than the clouds, lost in the air, banished to a place where no one could read him. What prompted his behavior towards me was the exile's fear that, without his photographs and the stories that accompanied them, I might not see him at all. Identity is more intricate than one imagines. In exile, it leaves no trace.

The myth of exile runs something like this. When someone goes to live in a foreign country, he can't take enough of the past with him to matter. In his own land, when someone sees him, even for a few minutes, he is more understood than he is in exile after twenty years. And so the exile begins to imagine the homeland as paradise and to inhabit it in his dreams.

But there is no coming home. Even if the house remains the same, those who live there grow and change. A person without a present doesn't exist at all. If a baggage handler isn't a baggage handler, then who is he? In resisting change, in arresting the flow of time and circumstance, an exile becomes fractured, a lost soul.

AT HAITI Transair, while we wait to board the plane, the mood is somber. The last three decades have demanded too much of Cubans, condemning them to a feeling of alienation wherever they are. Even a visit to the beloved island heightens their sense of exile. Dreams and illusions end there; the border between the place from which one sets out and the remembered homeland is always impossible to cross. Still, there are moments of belief—that the stars, the mountains, the palm trees will arrange themselves into a familiar composition; that relatives will embrace. Almost all of the travelers, people in late middle age whose faces show strain and fatigue, had emigrated from the island after the revolution. Their travels are invitations to confront painful realities. Who can call the island home? Doesn't Cuba belong exclusively to those who stayed behind? Does the past flow into the present?

Since Fidel Castro came to power, Cuba and the United States have glared at each other from opposite sides of the straits. In its old feud with Fidel, the United States has tried to strangle the Castro regime with an embargo. (Americans who travel to Cuba without a special license from the Treasury Department are "trading with the enemy.") Although the policy has caused hardship, it hasn't had the desired political effect. It has in fact unified those loyal to Castro, rallied them.

Cuba, too, is cruel and capricious. Fidel Castro attempts to decide who leaves his island, but he can be crossed. My own romantic favorite, Eugenio Maderal, windsurfed across the straits in nine hours, to arrive pained but unassisted on the beach at Marathon. Imagination, pluck, and spirit—freedom rides on rafts made from armoires, wooden surfboards, and hang gliders that would have impressed Leonardo—often succeed where leaden prohibitions fail. Strict regulations often breed fanciful evasions. The Havana hat ladies are famous as intrepid travelers who defeat the government-imposed weight limits with ingenuity, a straw hat, and a sewing kit. ("They never weigh what you're actually wearing.") The large woman in front of me has secreted in the headband of her hat: a few bars of chocolate, a red brush, a comb, many ropes of pearls, and lipsticks tied into the straw with grosgrain ribbons.

The passengers release tension in stories about their problems. A red-faced man in cordovan boots frets over his cache of dental supplies. With a suitcase full of them, donations to a clinic in Santiago, he's over the baggage limit unless he can prove that the delicate drills are medical supplies not covered by the rules. A middle-aged woman, frosted hair like a helmet, explains that she was an art historian in Havana but is now a manicurist in Miami. *"Cada día, la lucha."* ("Every day, the struggle.") For the children who must be educated, she goes to battle against broken nails.

A Californian who knows only a few words of English opens his briefcase so that we are able to see the hundred pairs of glasses with which he returns to a village near Holguín. I envision the arrival at his father's house. Word spreads; neighbors embrace him. The man, the beloved son who brings the fatted calf, sits down at his father's table. And he cries, even here he cries, because he can't do more.

A young girl in designer jeans and cowboy boots tells me that she's employed as a secretary. Her last visit to Havana to see her family cost her almost five thousand dollars. She even had to buy a refrigerator for her aunt's house in Camagüey. If she doesn't return, she'll be riddled with guilt and feel that she hasn't a family. *Los gusanos* who abandoned Cuba now return bearing gifts, like gilded *mariposas* (butterflies).

A man sitting on his suitcase invites me to examine his map of Cuba. With his hand, he traces the island's undulating curves. In the 1950s, American visitors to Havana bought handbags decorated with the heads of crocodiles. I remember seeing a battalion of defeated reptiles, forced from their lairs into glass presentation cases, glaring at the hordes of tourists.

Finally, we are in the air. Neither government can change the nature of the hour's voyage across the sun-dappled waters, nor can politics compromise its pleasures. The Straits of

Florida—the shark-infested, ninety-mile barrier between two countries—seem inviting, as though they had reverted to form and were once again the entrance gates to a fabled island.

AT NATY'S stone house, Doña Natica enters the living room, pauses at the chair in front of the television, and eases herself into her seat; distant and regal, she receives me as though I had asked for an audience. When Naty leaves the room, she whispers to me: "Fidel finished us off." With those words, Doña Natica straightens her back and assumes the posture of an empress in exile: the proud Czarina Alexandra, perhaps, under house arrest.

Soon she drifts into the past. In the early fifties, she announces with relish, when Fidel Castro was in the mountains (and no one in Havana thought to have anything to do with him), Doña Natica was asked to give a dinner at Naty's house. Her son-in-law, Orlando Fernández, had wanted to impress some of his international colleagues. Her daughter had no time for any of that, even then.

But Doña Natica was delighted to arrange the affair, choosing the white tablecloth embroidered in lace, noting with pleasure the English silver which gleamed from the polished sideboards. And how she remembers the food on that occasion, the croquettes of ham, the roast loin of pork, the avocado-and-mango salad. For dessert, Doña Natica had served a traditional Cuban flan, a wonderful caramelized custard. Everyone had loved it, particularly the Mexican cardiologist, who, she learned later, was also a Communist. Some of Doña Natica's favorite stories concern Communists who have a secret taste for elaborate capitalist dinners.

The television flickers on in time for her to catch the very end of the Brazilian *telenovela*. I'm reminded of warm after-noons in which (eluding my grandmother) I had sat in Tía Antonia's kitchen listening to the *radionovelas* with the cook: "La Serpiente Roja" with the fabulous detective Chan Li Po, "El Collar de Lágrimas," and "El Derecho de Nacer"—a drama so convincing that I decided to change my name to that of the heroine, Isabel Cristina.

The saga of Naty Revuelta and her family brought me back into that lugubrious afternoon world: the angry, narrow quar-rels between mothers and daughters, the excitement of illicit lovers, the challenge of eroticism, the search for a father, the doomed romanticism of it all.

Naty enters the room. "Can we get the garden wall fixed?" Doña Natica asks. "That's not possible," answers her daughter, "the government only repairs national monuments." "But that's fine," her mother answers: *"We* are the national monuments."

IN HAVANA, along the Malecón, young dreamers stare out to sea. A storm nears; it's beginning to rain very hard. The blackening water churns, waves crash and slam against the sea-wall. It's a powerful reminder that Havana is built on an island, and that it depends for its survival on the compact it makes with generations of traders, and also with the sea.

What, after all, does one family's story matter? It seems so insignificant alongside the larger tale of ambition, power, and greed buried in the stones of this four-hundred-year-old city. Isn't that what drove the Spanish to abandon small towns in Galicia and Andalusia and brave the ocean in uncomfortable wooden boats? Didn't the Midas promise prompt the voyages of French pirates, English sailors, American sugar barons, and mobsters from Chicago and Las Vegas?

I turn some of the stories around in my mind. Hatuey, the Indian chief resisting the arrival of Diego Velázquez, the conquistador who sent the Indians to the rivers to pan for gold: "These Europeans worship a very covetous sort of God. They will exact immense treasure of us and will use their utmost endeavors to reduce us to a miserable state of slavery or else put us to death." About to be burned at the stake, Hatuey was asked whether he might not want to convert to Catholicism so that he might claim a place in heaven. "Will there be Spaniards there?" he asked. Told that the Spanish would be well represented, he declined the offer of immortality. Perhaps the thoughtful leader was the first Cuban to resist strange gods. Certainly, he provided a model for resistance to the demands of treasure hunters willing to impose their truths with bludgeons.

It's hard not to look at Cuba in allegorical terms, as the noble, beleaguered Indian leader who wanted the outside world to leave him alone. But a pattern of invasion established itself. Fidel Castro is not so different from the conquistador Diego Velázquez. Fidel, too, has wanted Cuba to serve his own gods: *"Dentro de la revolución, todo; contra la revolucíon, nada."* ("Within the revolution, everything; outside the revolution, nothing.") Too few people knew that when Fidel first marched into Havana. For many Cubans in that time of innocence— Naty Revuelta included—there was a patriotic, populist impulse behind the enthusiasm for Fidel's revolution. "That's what the Americans can't forgive us," Fidel said before the Bay of Pigs, "that we've had a socialist revolution right in front of their noses." By then, he, too, had turned into Hatuey's nightmare.

IT SEEMED as though these tales of power and adventure were all there ever was. But when I visited Naty again—a woman whose daughters were lost to her—I realized that I couldn't use these stories or this theme to make sense of her life. Standing there, her stone house in darkness, the carved wooden chairs sagging, the china hidden in the closets, the photographs fading in their frames, the doors locked and the windows closed, she seemed, in herself, to represent longing, separation, and the pain of exile.

Another story of Cuba crossed my mind, but I had to turn it around so that the main character faded into the background. In the account of Hernando de Soto's historical travels, I unearthed some passages about his wife, Isabela de Bobadilla—a minor figure, who patiently waited for her husband's return to Havana from the wilds of Florida. (It's thought that *La Giraldilla*, the statue that represents Havana, is, in fact, the patient Isabela.)

It was a simple tale. After de Soto landed in Cuba, he discovered that there was no gold on the island. Completely disillusioned with his prospects, the resourceful adventurer climbed into his boat, crossed the straits, and headed for what is now Tampa Bay. Isabela de Bobadilla would never see her husband again, for, after his discovery of the Mississippi River, he caught a fever and died.

For three years, Isabela de Bobadilla had climbed the steep steps to the watchtower of the Castillo Real de la Fuerza and scanned the seas in search of de Soto. The poignant image of Isabela at the watchtower, patiently awaiting a reunion with her husband, has its modern analogue. At this moment in Cuba's history, so familiar is her figure that it seems pressed into the very stones of Havana—an image of hopeless separation rendered over and over again.

Those who suffered most in Cuba were not the leaders, who, after all, followed their stars. History would take care of Hernando de Soto and Fidel Castro. Those who endured hard times were simpler folk who were hostage to other people's dreams. The story of Naty Revuelta, the saga of her family, teaches us about them, and the dreadful effect of history upon ordinary life. Her story is about Isabela alone in her tower, not about Hernando de Soto.

In the best of times, history is gentle; in Cuba, it has been severe. Doña Natica has been the most vulnerable member of her family. It wouldn't have been easy for her to choose exile, because she hadn't the resources to take care of herself. She had nothing but her family, and she might never see her two granddaughters again, never see their children married. Her Meissen cake plates, the crystal goblets were worthless artifacts, as discredited as the Shroud of Turin.

Of the five women, probably Nina is the most fortunate. She gained entrance into the New World and, in her own way, is thriving. Still, the revolution has drained even her. She watched her father struggle to establish himself while caring for her; she's suffered an irrevocable separation from her mother and her sister.

Alina has suffered the most emotional damage, wandering alone, bewildered, lashing out at friend and enemy alike. What to do with her life? The unacknowledged daughter of the man who transformed both her country and her family, she acts, much of the time, like a wild child lost in a fun house.

But I think most about the effect of history on Naty. Fidel's judgment of her was facile, dismissive: "Naty missed the train." But what train? Wasn't it his train, not hers? And he, too, was now in trouble, spellbound by his empty rhetoric, waving at crowds that weren't there. He was like Napoleon on St. Helena, a prisoner playing on the floor with tin soldiers, re-creating his victories in battles ended long ago.

Naty, the beautiful woman who insisted on staying behind, waiting for Fidel, is the most accessible image of the failed

Doña Natica reminding me that she resembles
Queen Elizabeth, 1992

Doña Natica at home, watching television

promise, the ruin of the revolution. Her illusions had dominated her life, had kept her believing in Fidel. But even for her, the dream is now over. She has sacrificed four decades for a man and a movement that gave her nothing. There is no trace of humor when she talks about that long episode, and yet, miraculously, none of the bitterness that I had assumed would lodge inside her.

An incurable romantic, Naty cannot live without believing in someone. Once it was Fidel Castro; now it's Mumín, her granddaughter. She is preparing her house for the imagined return of Mumín from Miami—for that time when history, as it must, sees Fidel removed from the island.

Naty is right to shift her attention. Cuba, whatever she will be, no longer takes the measure of herself from Fidel Castro. A generation with designs of its own is replacing both antagonistic exiles and supporters of his fading regime. There's nothing in the argument between the two sides that matters except the opportunity it presents for forgiveness.

WALKING along the Malecón, I linger at a marble column on which a taloned bronze eagle once stood. It was a monument to the Americans on board the SS *Maine* who died fighting for the Cubans during their war for independence. After the Castro revolution, anti-American demonstrators knocked the eagle from its stand. Fidel Castro asked Picasso to replace the eagle with a dove. The artist refused, insisting that he couldn't top a neoclassical column with a cubist bird. It seems just as well, since it goes against the Cubans' grain to accept the eagles or doves of any country but their own. Isn't that what all their revolutions had been about? I imagine, instead, a Cuban bird alighting on that column—a descendant, perhaps, of one

Naty, at sixty-seven

Columbus might have heard singing when he sailed into the harbor.

My thoughts return to Naty—that proud, unbroken figure. I had started with only curiosity about her and come to feel nothing but compassion. Naty had smiled when I asked her about the future. She recited a Cuban proverb: *"No hay mal que dure cien años ni cuerpo que lo resista."* ("No evil lasts a hundred years, for no one exists who could live through it.") As I continued to walk along the Malecón, the warm rain that had been falling suddenly stopped. The light changed; the splendid island glistened in the sun.

SELECTED CHRONOLOGY

circa 1460   The Taino, a branch of the Arawak Indians from the Antilles, settle in Cuba, where they live in *bohíos* (palm-and-bamboo huts), sleep on *hamacas* (hammocks), and smoke a burning weed called tobacco.

1492   Christopher Columbus, having sailed for Asia, reaches the island of Cuba. A stubborn man, he insists that when the "Indians" talk about Cuba, they must mean Cipango, Marco Polo's name for Japan. Convinced that he's been to Asia, Columbus requires sailors on his second voyage to swear that Cuba isn't an island but, rather, the beginning of the "Indies." To Cuba he brings fruits, livestock, vegetables—and, more important, sugar cane.

1511   Diego Velázquez, appointed governor of Cuba, begins the Spanish Conquest. He lands in Baracoa, on the eastern end of the island, and founds the first permanent European settlement. On his orders, Hatuey, the Taino Indian leader, is tortured and burned at the stake.

1515   Diego Velázquez founds seven towns, including San Cristóbal de La Habana. When that town is moved to its present site, it's renamed Puerto Carenas. In 1538, the town is again called San Cristóbal de La Habana and becomes the capital of Cuba.

1539   Fearful of treasure-mad pirates attacking the Spanish, Hernando de Soto orders the construction of the Castillo Real de la Fuerza to protect Havana.

Selected Chronology

1590   Two new fortresses are built in Havana: Castillos del Morro and de la Punta. The city fathers issue a decree against the butchering of turtles and the preparation of *tasajo* (jerked beef) within the city limits.

1622   A Caribbean hurricane destroys the entire Spanish treasure fleet off the coast of Florida, including the *Atocha*.

1634   The King of Spain declares Havana "Key to the New World and Bulwark of the West Indies."

1674   Havana begins construction of her defensive city walls; they would take over a century to complete and would stand until 1863. The walls fostered the sense of the island as a dangerous place, with only a strong citadel in its midst to provide safety.

1728   The University of Havana is founded. Excluded from attending are *mulatos* and Negroes, Jews, and Moors.

1762   The British, under Lord Albemarle, capture Havana. In their eleven months of occupation, they open the port to foreign trade. (Havana had previously traded with Spain alone.) Thousands of slaves are imported to work on the sugar plantations. Cuba is transformed into a rich sugar island dominated by a titled *criollo* (native-born) oligarchy.

1812   The Spanish introduce Cubans to the lottery.

1823   John Quincy Adams establishes the U.S. position of "entitlement" towards Cuba. "There are laws of political as well as of physical gravitation; and if an apple, severed by the tempest from its native tree, can not choose but fall to the ground, Cuba, forcibly disjoined from its unnatural connection with Spain and incapable of self-support, can gravitate only toward the North American Union, which, by the same law of nature, can not cast her off from its bosom."

1839   In Havana, the Cuban Antonio Meucci is said to have invented the telephone and had his patent stolen by an American in New York City.

1840   Doña Mercedes de Santa Cruz, Condesa de Merlín, visits her native Havana. In her family home, she is attended by a hundred slaves.

Selected Chronology

1864   Herbert Acton Clews, Doña Natica's father, is born in England.

1868   Carlos Manuel de Céspedes, an enlightened landowner educated in Barcelona, liberates the slaves on his Cuban plantation and calls for revolution—start of "the Ten Years War" (the earliest bid for Cuban independence), which ends with the unfortunate Treaty of Zanjón.

1881   Dr. Carlos Finlay, an eminent Cuban doctor, announces his theory that mosquitoes cause yellow fever.

1894   Herbert Clews, naval engineer, arrives in Havana.

1898   On February 15, 1898, the U.S. battleship *Maine* is blown to pieces in Havana Harbor. "Stay there," William Randolph Hearst had wired Richard Harding Davis and cartoonist Frederic Remington in Havana. "You furnish the pictures and I'll furnish the war." On January 1, 1899, having signed the Treaty of Paris, the Spanish leave Cuba to the mercy of the Americans.

1900   Birth of Doña Natica Clews.

1901   The Platt Amendment is signed, giving the U.S. the right to intervene in all Cuban affairs. After Cuba's independence from Spain, American money starts to dominate the sugar industry. Cuba develops a one-crop economy which depends for its health on the fluctuations of the price of sugar. (By 1958, Americans own 121 of the 161 sugar mills on the island.)

1903   The United States establishes a naval base in Guantánamo Province, on the eastern end of the island. It will be a permanent thorn in Fidel Castro's side, particularly when military maneuvers are staged there.

1921   José Raúl Capablanca, the Cuban grand master, wins the World Chess Title; he holds on to it for six years.

1924   Doña Natica Clews marries Manolo Revuelta.

1925   General Gerardo Machado becomes president of Cuba; he begins the process of transforming himself from a war hero into a ruthless dictator. In 1933, after an army revolt, he's overthrown and retires to Miami Beach.

1925 Birth of Natalia (Naty) Revuelta Clews.

1926 Birth of Fidel Castro.

1927 Langston Hughes, the American poet, visits Havana.

1928 American industrialist Irenee Dupont buys hundreds of acres of land at Varadero Beach and builds himself a dream house called Xanadu. In the 1990s, the opulent house will be popular with posing bridal couples.

1929 Doña Natica and Manolo Revuelta divorce.

1930 Albert Einstein visits Havana. He is honored by the Cuban Academy of Sciences and buys a hat at El Encanto, the famous department store.

1931 Death of Herbert Clews.

1932 Ernest Hemingway sets out for Havana. He's accompanied by his friend Joe Russell, owner of Sloppy Joe's bar. Hemingway rents a room in the Hotel Ambos Mundos. In the mornings, he fishes for marlin. In the afternoons, he writes stories and reads the galley proofs of *Death in the Afternoon*.

1935 Doña Natica marries Herberto Coll.

1946 The Cuban Aviation Company inaugurates the first daily flights between Havana and Miami.

1948 Naty marries Dr. Orlando Fernández Ferrer. A year later, their daughter, Nina, is born.

1952 General Fulgencio Batista takes over the Cuban government in a coup d'état.

1953 On July 26, 1953, Fidel Castro attacks the army garrison at Moncada. He's captured and sent to prison on the Isle of Pines.

1956 Birth of Alina Fernández Revuelta.

1958 On New Year's Eve, General Batista's regime collapses; the dictator flees to the Dominican Republic.

1959   Fidel Castro's triumphant march into Havana.

1960   Cuba moves towards the Soviet Union. A Castro biographer describes the propagandist's attempt to ban Santa Claus. A revolutionary figure named "Don Feliciano" took his place, and a popular American tune re-emerged equipped with new lyrics: "Jingle bells, jingle bells, always with Fidel."

1961   The Bay of Pigs Invasion, sponsored by the United States, ends in disaster. The U.S. breaks off diplomatic relations with Cuba and declares a trade embargo. A victorious Fidel Castro declares himself to be a Marxist-Leninist.

1962   President John F. Kennedy declares a total embargo on trade with Cuba.

The Cuban Missile Crisis. President Kennedy demands that the Soviet Union remove the nuclear missiles and bombers it has introduced into Cuba. After twelve days of crisis, Soviet leader Nikita Khrushchev agrees to withdraw them in return for a U.S. promise not to invade Cuba. Fidel Castro is humiliated by having been treated as a pawn by the superpowers.

1967   Death of Che Guevara in the Bolivian jungle. With him goes the "romance" of the revolution.

1968   Small private businesses are confiscated. Havana begins to lose her glamour. How can there be a "Paris of the Caribbean" without street vendors and outdoor cafés?

1970   "The year of the ten million tons." Fidel had the romantic belief—despite warnings from agricultural experts—that the country could produce a giant sugar harvest. It was a disaster.

1977   Birth of Mumin Salgado, Alina's daughter.

1980   Ten thousand Cuban refugees seek asylum in the Peruvian Embassy in Havana—the beginning of a mass exodus to the United States.

1981   Felix Fidel Castro Díaz, Fidel's only legitimate child, becomes the director of the Cuban Atomic Energy Commission.

1989   The fall of the Soviet Union devastates the Cuban economy, which has depended upon its subsidies.

1993   Alina Fernández Revuelta leaves Cuba. Twelve days later, on New Year's Eve, her daughter, Mumín Salgado, follows her into exile.

1997   Fidel Castro announces that, in celebration of the Pope's expected visit to Cuba in January, he has reinstated Christmas—at least for this year.

AUTHOR'S NOTE

MY FIRST meeting with Naty Revuelta was, of course, the impulse behind the writing of a story about Cuba—one that touched on the events of the last hundred years as experienced by one bourgeois family. In the interest of the narrative, I have compressed many visits to Cuba into three. I have also changed the names of several characters, including Naty's elder daughter, at their request or for their own protection. Sparksburg, Illinois, does not exist, but all of the other place names are real. I should note that "Natty," as Fidel addresses her in the letters, once spelled her name with two "t"s.

I am indebted to so many books and periodicals that it's impossible to list them all. But I couldn't have written the book without Hugh Thomas's *Cuba: The Pursuit of Freedom* (New York: Harper & Row, 1971). I am also grateful to have been able to use the following sources:

Albo, Emma Álvarez-Tabío. *Vida, Mansión y Muerte de la Burguesía Cubana*. Havana: Editorial Letras Cubanas, 1989.

Atkins, Edwin F. *Sixty Years in Cuba*. Cambridge, Mass.: Riverside Press, 1926.

Barclay, Juliette. *Havana: Portrait of a City*. London: Cassell, 1993.

Benítez-Rojo, Antonio. *The Repeating Island: The Caribbean and the Post-modern Perspective*. Durham, N.C.: Duke University Press, 1992.

Bourne, Peter. *Castro: A Biography of Fidel Castro.* New York: Dodd, Mead, 1986.

Canizares, Raúl. *Walking with the Night: The Afro-Cuban World of Santería.* Rochester, Vt.: Destiny Books, 1993.

Fergusson, Edna. *Cuba.* New York: Alfred A. Knopf, 1946.

Franqui, Carlos. *Diary of the Cuban Revolution.* New York: Viking Press, 1980.

Hergesheimer, Joseph. *San Cristóbal de La Habana.* New York: Alfred A. Knopf, 1927.

Hermer, Consuelo, and Marjorie May. *Havana Mañana: A Guide to Cuba and the Cubans.* New York: Random House, 1941.

Martí, José. *Inside the Monster: Writings on the United States and American Imperialism.* New York: Monthly Review Press, 1975.

Phillips, Ruby Hart. *Cuba: Island of Paradox.* New York: McDowell, Obolensky, 1959.

Quirk, Raymond. *Fidel Castro: The Full Story of His Rise to Power, His Regime, His Allies, and His Adversaries.* New York: W. W. Norton, 1993.

Rougemont, Denis de. *Love in the Western World.* New York: Pantheon Books, 1940.

Santa Cruz, Mercedes, Condesa de Merlín. *La Habana.* Miami: Ediciones Universal, 1981 (orig. 1844).

Stout, Nancy, and Jorge Rigau. *Havana.* New York: Rizzoli, 1994.

Szulc, Tad. *Fidel: A Critical Portrait.* New York: William Morrow, 1986.

Terry, T. Philip. *Terry's Guide to Cuba.* Boston: Houghton Mifflin, 1926.

Williams, Eric. *From Columbus to Castro: The History of the Caribbean.* New York: Random House, 1970.

Wright, I. A. *The Early History of Cuba: 1492–1586.* New York: Macmillan, 1916.

Through the Cuban Interests Section at the Swiss Embassy in Washington, D.C., I applied for an interview with Fidel Castro. My letter was never answered.

ACKNOWLEDGMENTS

THIS book would not have been possible without the assistance of many people, particularly in New York, Havana, and Miami. For their early encouragement, I would first like to thank Natalia Revuelta Clews and her family. For his remarkable generosity, I want to acknowledge Osvaldo Rodríguez, who spent many hours sharing his childhood memories of Alina Fernández and, later, re-creating the story of her "escape" from Havana. For their careful, insightful reading of the letters between Fidel and Naty, I am indebted to Marcia Welles and Ida Nicolaisen. I am also immensely grateful to Eileen Blumenthal, Herb Leibowitz, and Pat Strachan, who commented on every page of the manuscript and made invaluable suggestions.

On both sides of the Straits of Florida, many people generously shared their knowledge of Cuba, their family memories, their photographs, their tales of the island then and now: Walter Arensberg, Natalia Bolívar Arostegui, Nelia Barletta de Cates, Monsignor Carlos Manuel de Céspedes, Mario Coyula, Annamaría Crossfield, Fernando Espineira, Tita Fernández, Juana Fredes, Nena Mañach Goodman, Reynaldo González, the late Tomás Gutiérrez Alea, Helena Hackley, Roy Hoffman, Mirta Ibarra, Guillermo Jiménez, Craig Kayser, Zoila Lapique, María Luisa Lobo, Raúl and Ninón Rodríguez, Wayne Smith, Jorge Tabío, and translator Magda Vergara.

Throughout the writing of the book, other good friends encouraged me, supported me, and surrounded me with affection. For contributions ranging from late-night phone calls and discussions about passion and politics, to SoHo dinners and walks on Vineyard beaches, I am grateful to Terry Albright, Angelica Baird, Hillary Blocksom, Benita Eisler, Colin Eisler, Yasmine Ergas, Lucinda Franks, Lorna Goodman, Myrna Greenberg, Mac Griswold, Elizabeth Hawes, Marina Kaufman, Susana Leval, Pierre Leval, Phyllis Rose, Martha Saxton, Jean Strouse, Kathleen Sullivan, Judith Thurman, Jean-Claude van Itallie, Jeannette Watson, and Susan Yankowitz.

At Alfred A. Knopf, I want to thank Sonny Mehta, my publisher, and Carol Janeway, my editor—magicians both. They were there to make me believe I could pull this book out of the hat, and to show me how to do it. Stephanie Koven, Sophie Cottrell, and Karen Mugler were unfailingly attentive and generous as they guided the book through production. I appreciate also the encouragement of my wonderful agent, Gloria Loomis, whose enthusiasm for her writers is matched only by her passion for their work.

For several years, my family has endured the shifting currents that surrounded the creation of this tale about Cuba. For swimming with me while I worked to get my bearings, I am grateful to Barbara Gimbel, who has so lovingly taken me on as a daughter, and to my father, Roberto Rendueles Alsina, who first told me about Spain's adventures in the Caribbean.

For their caring support, I would like to thank my son David, and Stephanie Tayengco; my loving gratitude also to my son Mark and daughter-in-law Dede Welles, who brought their perceptive comments to bear on many versions of the manuscript. I'd also like to thank my stepson, Andrew Liebhafsky, and his wife, Mimi Rocah.

My husband, Doug Liebhafsky, who has labored over each revision, is as familiar with this book as I am. I thank him for his all-enabling love—and for the intelligence, the humor, and the integrity that color the landscape of the country we inhabit together.

ALONE OF ALL HER SEX
The Myth and the Cult of the Virgin Mary
by Marina Warner

Exploring the various roles Mary has assumed—Virgin, Queen, Bride, Mother, Intercessor—and drawing on various disciplines, Marina Warner shows how the figure of Mary has shaped and been shaped by changing social and historical circumstances from the first century to the present day.

History/0-394-71155-6

BLACK WOMEN IN WHITE AMERICA
A Documentary History
edited by Gerda Lerner

Slaves and school teachers, political activists and domestic servants, factory workers and philanthropic club women relate their own histories and the larger experience of their race and gender in this brilliantly researched and moving anthology.

Women's Studies/African-American Studies/0-679-74314-6

THE DEVIL IN THE SHAPE OF A WOMAN
Witchcraft in Colonial New England
by Carol F. Karlsen

In this provocative study, Carol F. Karlsen examines a society in which fears of witchery and witch hunts helped reinforce the status quo and reflected deeper sexual, religious, and economic tensions.

History/Women's Studies/0-679-72184-3

FEMINISM
The Essential Historical Writings
edited by Miriam Schneir

This richly diverse collection traces the path of women's struggle for freedom from the time of the American Revolution to the years after World War I. This seminal work includes excerpts from authors ranging from Mary Wollstonecraft to Virginia Woolf.

Women's Studies/History/0-679-75381-8

FEMINISM IN OUR TIME
*The Essential Writings
from World War II to the Present*
edited by Miriam Schneir

Here are the writings that inspired and continue to shape contemporary feminism as the source of the most profound social change in the world today. Beginning with the trailblazing works of Simone de Beauvoir, Doris Lessing, and Betty Friedan, *Feminism in Our Time* charts the women's movement to the present day.

Women's Studies/History/0-679-74508-4

LABOR OF LOVE, LABOR OF SORROW
*Black Women, Work and the Family,
from Slavery to the Present*
by Jacqueline Jones

"A seminal work of scholarship, which has no rival."
—Henry Louis Gates, Jr.

Labor of Love, Labor of Sorrow offers a powerful account of the changing role of American black women, in the labor force and in the family.

Winner of the Bancroft Prize
Social History/0-394-74536-1

A MIDWIFE'S TALE
*The Life of Martha Ballard,
Based on Her Diary, 1785–1812*
by Laurel Thatcher Ulrich

A Midwife's Tale tells the story of midwife and healer Martha Ballard, who kept a diary that recorded her arduous work as well as her domestic life in eighteenth-century Maine.

*Winner of the Pulitzer Prize
and the Bancroft Prize*
American History/Women's Studies/0-679-73376-0

ALSO AVAILABLE:
Good Wives/0-679-73257-8

REFUGE

An Unnatural History of Family and Place

by Terry Tempest Williams

Through tragedies both personal and environmental, Utah-born naturalist Terry Tempest Williams creates a document of renewal and spiritual grace that is a moving meditation on nature, women, and grieving.

Women's Studies/Nature/0-679-74024-4

THE ROAD FROM COORAIN

by Jill Ker Conway

A remarkable woman's clear-sighted memoir of growing up Australian: from the vastness of a sheep station in the outback to the stifling propriety of postwar Sydney; from an untutored childhood to a life in academia; and from the shelter of a protective family to the lessons of independence.

Autobiography/0-679-72436-2

THE SECOND SEX

by Simone de Beauvoir

Drawing on extensive interviews with women of every age and station of life, masterfully synthesizing research about women's historic and economic roles, *The Second Sex* is an encyclopedic and brilliantly argued document of inequality and enforced "otherness."

Women's Studies/0-679-72451-6

SISTERHOOD IS POWERFUL

An Anthology of Writings From the Liberation Movement

Edited by Robin Morgan

This anthology is a comprehensive collection of writings from the women's liberation movement, including articles, poems, photographs, and manifestos.

Current Events/0-394-70539-4

VAMPS AND TRAMPS
New Essays
by Camille Paglia

In this unfettered book of essays, Camille Paglia brings her visceral intelligence and sizzling rhetoric to bear on subjects that range from Bill and Hillary Clinton to Madonna, from Frankenstein to the novels of D. H. Lawrence, and from feminist icon Catharine MacKinnon to First Amendment flasher Howard Stern.

Essays/Popular Culture/0-679-75120-3

ALSO AVAILABLE :
Sexual Personae/0-679-73579-8
Sex, Art, and American Culture/0-679-74101-1

THE WEAKER VESSEL
by Antonia Fraser

Using the firsthand testimony of letters, journals, and period documents, this monumental nationwide bestseller is "an almost encyclopedic chronicle of women in 17th-century England . . . wives, warriors, heiresses, preachers . . . alive with anecdote after anecdote." —*The New York Times Book Review*

History/Women's Studies/0-394-73251-0

ALSO AVAILABLE :
The Warrior Queens/0-394-25932-7
The Wives of Henry VIII/0-679-73001-X

WOMEN, RACE AND CLASS
by Angela Davis

A powerful documented study of the women's movement in the U.S. from abolitionist days to the present that demonstrates how it has always been hampered by the racist and classist biases of its leaders.

Women's Studies/0-394-71351-6

ALSO AVAILABLE :
Women, Culture, and Politics/0-679-72487-7